AF539524

# The Holy of Holies

# Select Reviews

*"I had a chance to glance through the contents. I must commend you for the depth of your thinking and the liberated nature of your philosophy. I wish the publication to all success."*

*"I find your thoughts very unique and interesting. Off and on I open the book to read a chapter."*

- K.K. VENUGOPAL,
Attorney General for India

*"Thank you for the book 'The Holy of Holies' penned by you, which I found to be interesting."*

- A.M. KHANWILKAR,
Judge, Supreme Court of India

*"... your book 'The Holy of Holies' ... will have a place of pride in my collection."*

- UDAY U. LALIT,
Judge, Supreme Court of India

*"I express my immense pleasure to receive your book 'The Holy of Holies' a transgressing science and metaphysical philosophy and the depth of your thinking on every aspects of universal life. I convey my best wishes and acknowledge your book as a holy fame of philosophy to live and to live only."*

– BHUPENDRA PATEL,
Chief Minister, Gujarat State

*"A wonderful and a unique book 'The Holy of Holies' containing your philosophy regarding the Universe, Genesis of Life, the Concept of God etc... . I would love to read it. ... the book would certainly add something to my spititual life. I am very much impressed by your thought that 'the purpose of life is to live and live only."*

– PANKAJ MITHAL,
Chief Justice of the High Court of J&K and Ladakh

*"Upon perusing the contents of your book, titled The Holy of Holies, I would like to extend my heartfelt commendation for the profound intellect reflected in your work and the thought-provoking nature of your philosophical insights.*

*"I am truly impressed by the depth of your contemplation and the progressive ideals espoused throughout the book. I am confident that your publication will achieve significant recognition and triumph in the literary sphere."*

– DR. FAUZIA KHAN,
Member of Parliament (Rajya Sabha)

*"I compliment you for the work 'The Holy of Holies'. It is a scholarly work on philosophy, mythology, belief, and way of life. It's a phenomenal work, more particularly, because you are practising law and yet come out with a publication on a completely different subject, a combination of metaphysics, happiness, eternity, self-realization etc. Once I started reading the book, I completed the same with great interest."*

– VIJAY HANSARIA,
Senior Advocate, Supreme Court of India

*"A very thought provoking yet realistic assembly of your divine thoughts have been penned down in this book. Yes, I agree that this Universe runs on its own rules what may come and it is for us living beings to absorb the right kind of energies floating around us to make our journey in this world happy."*

– LALIT BHASIN,
Former President - Society of Indian Law Firms;
Bar Association of India; Indian Law Foundation; etc

*"The book, The Holy of Holies, will take you by surprise. It is a practical book on philosophy of life and living. The book unearths sufficient answers for many questions we invariably come across.... This will surely be a path-breaking book in its field."*

– SIDDHARTH SANGAL,
Advocate on Record, Supreme Court of India
Addl. Standing Counsel for the State of Uttarakhand

*"I also take this opportunity to congratulate you for the very meaningful and excellent book 'The Holy of Holies' authored by you. I was so elated to read the same that I twice ordered multiple copies of the book from amazon.com for my friends."*

– GAGAN ANAND,
Solicitor, England & Wales
Managing Partner, Legacy Law Offices

*"Didn't know that you are also a prolific writer with literary acumen, apart from legal acumen… this is just the beginning, you shall pen many more times."*

– AASHUTOSH JERATH,
Advocate, Punjab & Haryana High Court

*"पुस्तक में प्रयुक्त की गई भाषा एवं शैली अत्यन्त ही मार्मिक एवं हृदयस्पर्शी है। मैं आशा करता हूँ कि आपकी पुस्तक आम जन-मानस के लिए अत्यन्त ही रुचिकर एव प्रेरणादायी सिद्ध होगी।"*

– राजेन्द्र कुमार तिवारी
आई.ए.एस.,
अध्यक्ष, उत्तर प्रदेश राज्य सड़क परिवहन निगम

*"Topics related to everyday life and presented in a very concise and clear manner. This book is a starting point to deep dive further into this topic."*

– HIMANSHU MOHAN,
Director, Data Engineering Organisatin, Adidas India

*"The book is a masterpiece. These thoughts can only come out from good-hearted people. An amazing book, an eye opener towards philosophy of life & living."*

- DR. VIVEK AGGARWAL,
Renowned Endocrine Surgeon

*"I too had so many questions bothering me forever but after reading only a few pages of this great submission by you, I am sure I am going to get answers to most of the questions in my mind. And I think I would love to read this book again and again."*

- DR. ARCHANA ARYA,
Renowned Orthodontist

*"Your book is unque and discusses all the aspects of religion, spirituality and even prostitution. This book is for that class of people, who are unbiased and wish to shift the established angle of looking at things"*

- SUBODH GUPTA
Industrialist and Businessman

*"Your experience of the world, about happenings in world will guide not only this generation but perhaps generations to come."*

- INDU DAHUJA,
Housewife

The 'Certificate of Honour' presented to the Author by Hon'ble Dr. Justice D.Y. Chandrachud, The Chief Justice Of India, on the Law Day on November 25, 2022 for his book, 'The Holy of Holies', in presence of the President and Vice-President of Supreme Court Bar Association.

TILAK MARG, NEW DELHI - 110 001

**CERTIFICATE OF HONOUR**

*This is to Certify that*

*Mr./~~Ms~~.* ANIL KUMAR SANGAL (SR.) *is a member of the Supreme Court Bar Association and was honoured by the Chief Justice of India on the Law Day Function for authoring Book titled as* "The Holy of Holies The Theory of Everything as I understand it." *Dated this the* 25th *November, 2022.*

*President*
Vikas Singh (Sr.)
President
Supreme Court Bar Association

*Hony. Secretary*
RAHUL KAUSHIK

NATIONAL LAW DAY AWARD – 2022

INDIAN COUNCIL OF JURISTS

ALL INDIA BAR ASSOCIATION

Mr. Anil Kumar Sangal, Sr. Advocate is receiving National Law Day Award from Hon'ble Dr. Justice K.G. Balakrishnan, former Chief Justice of India and Hon'ble Dr. Adish Aggarwala, President, International Council of Jurists and Chairman, All India Bar Association in the presence of Hon'ble Dr. Indresh Kumar, Senior National Executive Committee Member of RSS; Hon'ble Mr. John F. Fernandes, Ex. Panel Vice Chairman of Rajya Sabha and Mr. Baldev Raj Mahajan, Sr. Advocate and Advocate General of Haryana; The citation reads "In recognition of his devotion to the study and practice of Civil, Service and Banking Laws. His exceptional dedication has aided in furthering the understanding of concepts involved in these Laws. also for authoring the book "Holy of Holies". A role model for the society." on November 25, 2022 at Plenary Hall of Indian Law Institute, Supreme Court of India, New Delhi.

(National Law Day Award-2022 Photo No. DSC_2169 dated 25.11.2022

The author was felicitated with National Law Day Award-2022 by Indian Council of Jurists and All India Bar Association on the Law Day on November 25, 2022, inter alia, for his book, 'The Holy of Holies'.

NATIONAL LAW DAY AWARD – 2022

PRESENTED TO

MR. ANIL KUMAR SANGAL

SENIOR ADVOCATE

BY

DR. JUSTICE K.G. BALAKRISHNAN

FORMER CHIEF JUSTICE OF INDIA

DR. ADISH C AGGARWALA

PRESIDENT, INTERNATIONAL COUNCIL OF JURISTS, LONDON

CHAIRMAN, ALL INDIA BAR ASSOCIATION

IN RECOGNITION OF HIS DEVOTION TO THE STUDY AND PRACTICE OF CIVIL, SERVICE AND BANKING LAWS. HIS EXCEPTIONAL DEDICATION HAS AIDED IN FURTHERING THE UNDERSTANDING OF CONCEPTS INVOLVED IN THESE LAWS. ALSO FOR AUTHORING THE BOOK "HOLY OF HOLIES". A ROLE MODEL FOR THE SOCIETY.

ON NOVEMBER 25, 2022 AT INDIAN LAW INSTITUTE, NEW DELHI

INDIAN COUNCIL OF JURISTS

ALL INDIA BAR ASSOCIATION

# The Holy of Holies

## The theory of everything as I understand

(A Metaphysical Philosophy Transgressing Nescience)

THIRD EDITION

2023

Anil Kumar Sangal

*(Swami Dhyan Utkarsh)*

Self-published:
ISBN 978-93-5493-511-4
First Edition, 2021
Second Edition (Paper back), 2022
Third Edition, 2023
Price: ₹ **550/-**

Cover Design : Divya Sangal
Proof Reading : Siddharth Sangal & Richa Mishra
Digital Layout : Sanjay Bhola 'Dheer'

Printed in India by:
Pushpak Press Pvt. Ltd., 203-204, DSIDC Sheds, Okhla Indl. Area Phase-I, New Delhi-110020. newpushpak@gmail.com

# CONTENTS

# FOREWORD

*K.K. Venugopal*
Attorney General for India

Supreme Court of India
New Delhi-110001
Tel: 23383254, 23070046
Fax: 23782101


To **July 4, 2021**

Shri Anil Kumar Sangal
Advocate-on-Record,
Supreme Court of India,
New Delhi

Dear Anil Kumar Sangal

Thank you for sending me a pre-publication copy of your book 'Holy of Holies'. I had a chance to glance through the contents. I must commend you for the depth of your thinking and the liberated nature of your philosophy. I wish the publication to all success.

(K.K. Venugopal)
Attorny General for India

*अंदाज़-ए-बयाँ गरचे बहुत शोख़ नही है,*
*शायद कि उतर जाए तिरे दिल में मिरी बात।*

*-अल्लामा इकबाल*

*Although my expression is not sharp enough,*
*yet may be my words pierce your heart.*

*-Allama Iqbal*

# PREFACE AND PRELUDE

I was very anxious and inquisitive about every thing since childhood. This book was however inadvertent and not a delibrate composition. The whole book had in fact been written by me in my own hand by way of messages on my WhatsApp Group, "The Holy of Holies", over a period of time, which were so fondly preserved by one of the members of the Group, Shri Yogesh Mittal, on his Laptop, and were later on forwarded to me on my e-mail, with an earnest suggestion that I must altruistically publish them in the form of a book. Hence this book. I also owe my gratitude to

Shri Ashish Agrawal of M/s Pushpak Press Pvt. Ltd. for such nice printing and presentation of the book.

Meanwhile, I had also received a number of interesting Questions on my Group and answered them too, which were also preserved and made available to me by Shri Mittal; but I decided not to make them part of this book.

I have written the text of the topics of this book in the same order and sequence as they intuitively occurred to me at different times and on the authority of my metaphysical experience and insight about the unity of everyone and everything and the universe.

I do not know whether I am a theist, atheist or agnostic. It is for my readers to deem or determine.

A. K. Sangal

(Anil Kumar Sangal)

Author

Delhi, June 11, 2021

# PROLOGUE AND PROPHECY

There have always been from time immemorial some very intriguing questions which humankind wanted to know the answers of. Some of such pertinent questions in substance are, Who I am, What is the purpose of my life, Can I do anything to the things happening to me or around me, If anything in me survives my death, What is all this infinite around me, and the like.

There have not been any definite scientific answers to these questions so far; and, may be, the answers to these questions fall in realms of Metaphysics and Nescience.

So many 'Saints' and 'Sages' have tried to discover the answers to these questions by *jap-tap* and supposedly reached to certain conclusions (by various thought processes of conjectures, surmises or even hallucinations, etc).

Their conclusions were in fact vindication of their own respective ideology, philosophy or hypothesis by their own persistence, and which, in turn, converted into their own honest convictions (may be due to self-deception). Each of such convictions, gave rise to a faith or religion. This explains, how and why, there are so many religions and religious sects with different faiths and beliefs about the same thing.

This book seeks to address, inter alia, so many such questions.

*'The earth has music for those who listen.'*

*-William Shakespeare*

SERIES - 1

# The Universe

1. The Universe is self-created and self-evolved, and has not been created by any outside entity, because there is nothing beyond it.

2. The Universe is not a dead thing, it is a living organism, which acts and reacts to each and everything happening or being done within, by even our thoughts and sights on objects, living or dead.

3. Our thoughts and sights do affect not only the other persons, but even giant mountains and seas.

4. So the whole-sole thing that exists is the Universe, which is one-whole, like a living 'organism', which acts, reacts, and even responds, scientifically, in a defined manner, mindlessly and without any discretion, automatically, worship or no worship.

5. So, the Universe having formed on its own may also be appropriately nicknamed as *'Khuda'*.

6. Hence, the Universe reacts and responds to our Thoughts, Actions, Deeds, and Acts of Omission and Commission as per the Provisions of its fixed and rigid Laws (*Vidhi ka Vidhan*), without any discretion or discrimination, come what may.

SERIES - 2

# Origin of Universe

7. There is nothing but energy; so to say, all matter is energy.

8. In the beginning, even before the beginning of time and day & night, there was nothing but energy, which was conscious with a sense of being and full of feelings of bliss *(which is the relegate state, so many people on earth have been obtusely trying to achieve from time immemorial and even today in the name of so- called Moksh/ Mukti / Uddhaar / liberation / salvation &c. by abstruse Saadhna, Bhakti, Jap-Tap and what not, as if the Parmatma is an idiot to have created this miraculous Universe and this wonderful world).*

9. This beautiful Earth is the Crown of the Universe.

10. This stupendous World has evolved on this mesmerising Earth.

11. I have said, in the beginning, even before the beginning of time and day & night, there was nothing but energy, which was conscious with a sense of being and full of feelings of bliss, which can also be described as *Brahm.*

12. The *Brahm,* despite being all bliss, was depressed like a destitute from its monotony; and became desperate to love, play and be happy.

13. The *Brahm* had no material to do or create anything for a change and entertainment to end its monotony; and therefore it created this Universe (*Brahmand*) out of itself by compressing and consolidating itself into a solid mass (*Shiva*).

14. Then the *Brahm* separated itself from itself to love and enjoy itself; and exploded itself in a big bang; and the Universe (*Brahmand*) was formed. So, there is nothing but God.

15. Thus, the whole Universe, having formed from *Shiva,* is still a Unit and its conscious energy (conscience) runs it, which we can deem as its consort and name her as *Shakti.*

16. I have described above the Earth as the Crown of the Universe. The conscious energy of the Universe is today reflected in so many ways, like by friction, striking, lightening and is even obtaining as Electricity.

17. The residues of the conscious energy impregnated in solid mass of the Earth resurrected as *Vegetation* all over.

18. But the *Brahm,* as *Shiva* and its consort *Shakti,* as a unit, was still alone in the saddle.

SERIES - 3

# Genesis of Life

19. The Universe having formed with beautiful Earth and exotic *Vegetation* on its surface, Hills and in the Oceans, the Consciousness of the Universe (*Parmatma*), despite being happier and all bliss, was nonetheless rolling in the boredom of monotony.

(Even in today's World, if a person has everything he needs or wants, but has nothing to perform, achieve or accomplish, such person can't even know the pleasure, happiness or joy of achievement, accomplishment or victory, much less experiencing them)

20. So, the *Parmatm*a created innumerable animated things and objects on Earth from the

combination of elements of Earth (Shiva) and its consciousness (Shakti) and with each its such creation, He was more or less happy but was not glad enough so as to end His boredom of monotony.

21. Hence, ultimately, the *Parmatma* descended on Earth as *Humans* to live a varied and ever changing life as Men and Women; and the whole Universe helps and supports us, the Humans, in whatever we do, good or bad.

There is intelligence behind 'creation' is best manifested by segregation of sex in mammals as Male and Female, who are though completely separate and independent of each other, but are yet perfectly compatible and integrally complementary to each other for sex and progeny. The same intelligence is also behind all evolutions and adaptations.

22. Where are you searching the so-called God or for the *Tatwa Gyaan,* it is right here. You have to just wake up.

SERIES - 4

# The Creation

23. So, the Universe and this beautiful world are real, tangible, genuine and live.

24. We know that we like the most to love and play with our coequals. *Parmatma* had none to love and play with. Hence, the *Parmatma* (Conscience of the Universe) created and evolved us from His matter & mettle, after His own image and imagination, like Himself, replete with His all faculties, and has securely placed and packed our such subtle and delicate essence (*Atma*) in wonderfully structured live bodies called *humans.*

25. As a matter of fact, the *Parmatma* separated Himself from Himself to love and play with Himself ( ie., us ).

26. Our body ie., the Human Body, is the finest creation ever done or to be ever done from the substantive elements of Earth, which could be, possibly performed, only by the *midas* touch of *Parmatma.*

27. Please make no mistake; the Universe has evolved itself from within itself; there was no creator of it outside it, such as the so-called God, as is generally/commonly assumed or believed.

28. There is nobody such as the so-called God sitting anywhere in the Universe or outside it, who is running/ controlling or regulating the Universe or, for that matter, this World either. Were it so, the Rains would be on time and only where they were required; no Droughts or Floods; no extreme Pains and Miseries of the kind of *Nirbhaya,* could occur in the kind regime of the so-called all-mighty, omnipresent, omniscient and omnipotent God.

29. I would rather say with full emphasis on my command that the *Things Simply Happen,*

as a result of innumerable and infinite factors and causes and reasons, which is a matter of study of Metaphysics and is as on date in the realms of nescience.

30. Our individual acts and deeds (the so-called *Karms*) are of little significance vis-a-vis the Universe or even this World, except to ourselves; but our thoughts and intentions behind them, and also otherwise, are of tremendous effects and consequences on us, on our society, on this world and the whole Universe. So, let us consciously and deliberately develop and adopt the attitudes and demeanours of Love, Compassion and Joy towards one and all, come what may.

31. So, the *Parmatma* divided himself from himself to live in us and love and play and enjoy himself amongst us.

32. Now, therefore, it is upto us to allow the *Parmatma* to lead a life of love and enjoyment or to play the game of life with hatred, cruelty and deceit.

33. We the humans, having been made the same as the *Parmatma* himself, a complete freedom and liberties are naturally guaranteed to us.

34. We the humans, are thus the same as is the *Parmatma*. Some of us can realise it; and others may not even have any idea of it, much less realising this.

35. The consciousness of the *Parmatma* has resurrected and is indirectly reflected in the vegetation (*Vegetable Kingdom*) and is directly reflected in the animated creation (*Animal Kingdom*) while the *Parmatma* Himself is present in the *Mankind*.

36. So, we the humans, each of us, has the same sublime conscientiousness as is of the infinite *Parmatma*, within the confines and limitations of our respective bodies, yet with a terrific advantage of this puzzling Human Body, in which the *Parmatma* himself lives in us as our *Praan* and is reflected as our *Mann* through the mechanisms of the Brain (Nervous System).

37. So, nobody can ever catch, control or silence the *Mann per se*; stifling the Nervous System is a different matter.

38. The *Parmatma,* who dwells in us as our *Praan/Mann,* connects Himself to the outside World/Universe through our *Sense Organs,*

and He likes and enjoys the most the Beauty, the Love and the Sex.

SERIES - 5

# The Concept of God

39. The so-called God is not a thing or an entity but a concept.

40. And, if I say God knows, I mean: "I don't know" or "Nobody knows" or "It is unknown"; and, surely, it doesn't mean 'There's a God who knows it'.

41. And, "Oh my God", is merely an expression of exclamation and not an acknowledgment of existence of the entity of God of the kind it is generally believed or assumed.

42. In the context of the above, I may add that the word "God" may also be used as a synonym

of 'Universe' or 'Existence'; But mistake not, to take it to be something separate or somebody sitting somewhere in the skies.

43. So, the *Parmatma* is alive in us as our Atma in the form of our Consciousness, which reflects and registers its presence in us as our *Mann* (Our Inner Voice/*Anter Mann ki Awaaz*/*Ander ki Awaaz*/ Inner Feeling/Gut Feeling &c).

44. So, we, in essence, are nothing but a mere consciousness, with a *Mann* as its Voice of Silence, as per an individual's Intelligence and Talents.

45. Our individual Conscience evolves constantly, Good or Bad, getting Energy, more or less, from the Universe.

46. The *Mann* never dies/vanishes (I have personally experienced it twice). So, the good people will be better; and bad people will be worse, in their next reincarnations as humans.

47. We can't know or understand our *Mann* but we can certainly feel and experience its existence as "I", "Me" and what we may also call "Ego".

48. All of our Faculties are attributable to our *Mann*. We must not confuse or relate our Knowledge and Information with our Awareness, Intelligence and Talent but should rather try and contradistinguish them from each other.

49. That is why, you can easily find, so many uneducated, yet very intelligent and talented people, around you; and very many (I have avoided saying most) highly educated fools too. I have not included the 'idiots' in this category because I genuinely consider myself a 'First Class Idiot' and, nevertheless, I hold myself in high esteem.

50. We are constantly evolving as per our instincts and experiences, we want or don't; yet those who chance to realise their real sacred self, howsoever, attain *"Bhagwatta"* (self-realisation) and can evolve tremendously, in any fashion or manner, good or bad. Lord Ram and Lord Krashn are very good, or rather the best, examples of very highly evolved and pure (sacred) Humans.

SERIES - 6

# Self Realisation

51. So, I have explained very simply what really we in fact are; but even after genuinely understanding it, if at all, that we are nothing but mere consciousness, which is immortal and constantly evolves, better or worse, we want it or don't; yet, the self-realisation is not commonplace occurrence, in our lives.

52. The actualisation of realisation of our *"Sacred Self"* ie., attainment of *"Bhagwatta,"* may occur to anyone of us anytime and anywhere, with or without any effort; or it may not happen in life after life, even with all-out efforts and trying all sorts of means & measures.

53. The Self-Realisation is in fact the 'zenith' of humans' life and can also be termed as attainment of *"Moksh"*; and the *"Mukti"* (Freedom from Fear of Death) is its essential attribute and consequence.

54. The attainment of *Moksh* can lead to Salvation and may even make you Ram, Krashn or Budh; or may be disastrous for the society and may make you Rawan, Kans, or even Shakuni.

55. There are known common Faculties/ Abilities in a normal human being, but some people are extraordinary, and are gifted with some kind of special powers or skills. Such persons are in fact far more evolved than general public; and are in common parlance called *'Mahapurush'* or *'Mahamanav'*.

56. Some person(s) may sometimes be so much and so highly evolved that he is borne with, or attain to, supernatural powers and abilities. Such persons, who can do or perform what no normal/common man on Earth can, are deemed as "Incarnations"(*Avtaars*).

SERIES - 7

# Purpose of Life

57. So, we now revert to the purpose of life. It is certainly not renunciation from this wonderful body and life on this beautiful planet called Earth.

58. I don't know what kind of life or existence the people anticipate, after they get parablic *Mukti* (rid from the cycle of birth and death) and attain so-called *Moksh* (An exalted special status in skies).

59. In my view, the whole and sole purpose of life is to live and enjoy it, life after life; and to entertain ourselves with all kinds of *Rases* like *Prem Ras, Shringaar Ras, Bhakti Ras* or even

*Shok Ras* and *Raudra Ras*, through the amazing instrumentation of our Sense Organs.

60. Everything on this Earth and in this World is meant for us humans. Even if we kill an animal, its pain is only as much and like as we suffer in our dreams; the suffering of vegetables, which are also live, is far less than the animals. It is pertinent that only the live things can support life on Earth.

61. There is chasm of difference between the thinking, feelings, sensibility, sensitivity, perspectives & understanding of the Life, objects/purposes of Life, of a human who has attained *'Moksh'* (ie., Self-realisation) and those who don't have even ever thought or have an inkling as to what they are, much less knowing who they are.

62. Those humans who have realised their Sacred-Self, ie. those who have attained *'Moksh'*, get *'Mukti'*, perforce and *ipso facto*, automatically.

63. Those, who attain *Moksh*, evolve more (in dimensions) and very fast (speedily); and have even the potential of attaining the status

of so-called gods, like Lord Ram, Lord Krashn or Buddha the great.

64. But, more is anyone evolved, more and more intense is the feel of Pleasure and Pain; and at the same time, far more is the tolerance and sustainability.

65. The people who attain self-realisation ie., *Moksh*, become charismatic, magnetic, erudite and erogenous; and miracles start happening in their day-to-day life.

66. It is these people who appreciate and understand the importance of *"dharm"* in life for the sustenance and survival of an happy society, far more than any other people.

67. To me, the *'dharm'* means a way of life which ensures our mutual and equitable coexistence, welfare and happiness of one and all.

68. No worthy society can even survive without *dharm*, much less a loving society, having Peace and Happiness everywhere.

69. Without *dharm*, the whole human world would be bound to be devastated by

waywardness/contrariness/arbitrariness/despotism and the consequent selfish & ruthless fights for Wealth and Women; or at best, there will be a virtual anarchism with some kind of a despotic autocracy.

70. I consider the Law of the Land and the contemporary, prevailing Norms of demeanour & Etiquette of a Civilised Society, which are legitimate, just and reasonable, as an integral part of *'dharm'* itself.

71. What has our so-called God done on Earth so far, after its origin, without we or somebody doing anything.

72. I do not appreciate or can understand how our *Katha-Vachaks/Updeshaks*, who are shouting full throttle day-in and day-out to have faith in *Prabhu Ram* or *Prabhu Shyam* &c for anything and everything, can be of any help or service to the society in accomplishing anything, much less everything, except misleading us to the *Greatest Myth* that everything is done by God and whatever He does is good and always for our Good.

73. We see so often untimely rains, or no-rains, or floods, or famines, causing so much devastation to the people and to the crops and misery to the poor cultivators bulldozing their legitimate expectations, without any fault or folly of theirs.

74. How do we explain the events like *'Nirbhaya Kand'*, if the so-called God of the kind He is generally believed in, does/ witnesses everything and each happening. Let us assume, there were her own very bad, dirty or cruel deeds (*karms*) behind it, but then what about His projected and propagated goodwill and kindness, which is so widely professed over the Globe.

75. The gospel of *Prabhu/Ishwar/Bhagwan* has over a period become so heavy on our psyche that it has virtually captivated us and our mindset by His assumed awesome power, prowess and fear; and made us idiotically dependent on the myth of so-called God.

76. In my view, the reason behind this irrational, dangerous, devastating, and wasteful belief in the myth of the so-called God is that we don't know who we are :-

a) A very few people in their life question to themselves as to who they are.

b) A very few of 'them' try to know as to who they were. And

c) A rare ones of them are able to know their Sacred-Self ie., attain *Moksh* in life, and live a *Mukt* and beautiful life on Earth, now and here.

I am really very sorry and sad about ourselves, literate and illiterate alike. In fact the literate ones are more stubborn and difficult in this regard, like, *"know not, know not, know not"*.

SERIES - 8

# The 'Dharm'

77. I must clarify that learning about self-realisation is not the same thing as attaining self-realisation (*Bhagwatta*) and knowing your Sacred-Self, which ipso facto bestow *'Moksh'* and *'Mukti'* on the knower.

78. I have already emphasised the importance of *'dharm'* and that any worthy 'society' (or even mankind) can't exist without it.

79. No Peace, Pleasure or Joy is possible on Earth for the mankind unless there is an 'orderly society'; and there is no question of any orderly society without *dharm,* which is a sine-qua-non and has in fact descended on Earth with the *Mankind.*

80. There is nobody on Earth who doesn't know his *dharm* ie., *"SwaDharm"*. Our (including infants and even a nascent child) *Mann* (which is the feel of *Parmatma* in us) constantly tells and even reminds us, "What we should do and what not"; we listen to it or not.

81. What is the *dharm* of a Father vis-a-vis a Son, and vice-versa, is known to every Father before the Son was even born; same is true for all other relationships, be it Husband-Wife, Brother-Sister, or King and his Subject.

82. So, the *'dharm'* is in fact innate and divine, and is valid for ever for all situations.

83. Please mistake not, to compare and confuse it with nasty religions, which are rather largely responsible for the annihilating state of Nations, today.

84. This innate and divine *dharm,* as contra-distinguished from the Religions, which are partisan and biased and are brought and imposed from outside, is very aptly called *"Sanatan Dharm"*.

85. So, the *Sanatan Dharm* is not a Religion. It is something Eternal & Innate, which can have no beginning or end; but the same, as it is being, of late, practised by Hindus, can be, of course, called *Hindu Religion.*

86. The Hindus perceived and recognised the *Sanatan Dharm* since antiquity and adopted it from time immemorial. The association of the Hindus with *Sanatan Dharm* was so much and so deep that the Hindus were even known as *'Sanatanis'.*

87. Lord Ram and Lord Krashn were Hindus and practised *Sanatan Dharm,* honestly and at all costs. They were not the prophets who founded any *dharm.* They were of course the propounders and the proponents of the *Hindu Dharm.*

88. Then, some self-appointed and self-styled, so-called *Rishis* and *Mehrishis,* attempted to pen down the so dynamic a *Sanatan Dhar*m in *Granths* (Books), like, *Manusmrity.* Thus, the *Sanatan Dharm* was in the name of codifying it, tinkered with, and so many Myths, Surmises and *Karam-Kand* (Rituals) got associated with

it from time to time, giving rise to the present day *mythic Hindu Religion.*

89. The *dharm* is, what is innately and always true and correct, looked from whichever angle.

90. The *dharm* is not, and can never be, a constant; it is dynamic because it differs from situation to situation and there can be unimaginably innumerable fact-situations.

91. Thus, obviously, the *dharm* can't ever be fully or perfectly codified. For the same reason, no Legal System in the World is perfect or infallible, and (they) so often lead to injustices, sometimes even due to the shackles of Laws and Rules made there under, themselves.

92. The Religions, which have, by and large, done no service to the society, except wasting valuable time of the mankind, making them superstitious and dividing them on religious lines.

93. In ancient times, till even after the Christ in AD Era, it used to be believed that the Sun revolves around the Earth, albeit unscientifically, because it appeared to be so,

obviously. The scientist who first time found out that it was other way round, it is Earth which revolves around the Sun (and also on its Axis), was held guilty of Blasphemy by a guild of Church, and sentenced to death.

94. Similarly, in ancient times, the denizens of India earnestly believed (out of ignorance) that the *Holy Ganga* descended on Earth from the Skies, the sharp flow of which was borne by the Hair of Lord Shiva, and that the people living in Himalayas (*Devtaas*) magnanimously flew it on Earth as Ganges (including its Tributaries). Such religious belief still survives in Hindu Mythology; whereas the truth is, it enamates from melting of giant Glaciers in high reaches of Himalayas.

95. After watching *Shiv Puran, Vishnu Puran,* &c on TV, it is my firm conviction now that those dwelling in Himalayas were regarded as *'Devtas'*; those living in plains of Northern India were called *'Manav'*; and those who were residing in Southern India were deemed *'Asurs'*.

96. Those who were dwelling in Himalayas were ranked according to location, situation,

conditions and heights of the reach of the respective abodes in Himalayas. Lord Shiva's abode was in the highest reaches of Himalayas and he was therefore ranked the mighty, formidable and indomitable, *"Mahadev"*.

SERIES - 9

# We are Phenomenal

97. The whole Universe, including this magnificent Earth and this stunning and stupendous World, is the creation of *Parmatma*, but nonetheless He does not have the kind of wonderful body and amazing faculties as we the Humans have to enjoy ourselves.

98. So, the *Parmatma* enjoys this World as our *Mann* in us.

99. So, our *Mann* is the same matter and mettle as is the *Parmatma* Himself ie., the consciousness of the Universe.

100. I have no hesitation in saying that each one of us, in essence and as our Real-Self, is the same as were Lord Ram and Lord Krashn.

101. We have Eye-Sight to see and enjoy the beauty of nature, the beauty of creation, and the most, to witness the diversity of the beauty and dance of women, like the variety of flowers. It reminds me the proverbial *Darbar* of *Indra Dev* and the *'Muzra'* of yesteryears.

102. We have Ears to hear the musical sounds and voices of the nature, and to hear the sweet voices, melodious music and songs of ourselves.

103. We have Tongue to taste the delicious cuisines and help speak, sing, and have dialogue with ourselves.

104. We have Nose to sense decent scents of the nature and of our mates.

105. We have the sense of touch to feel a variety of emotions by touch; and the most, the experience of supreme pleasures of mating, called Sex.

106. The sense of Eyes (*sight*) is attributable to Fire; The sense of Ears (*sound*) is attributable to Ether/Sky; The sense of Tongue (*taste*) is attributable to Water; The sense of Nose (*odour*) is attributable to Earth; and the sense of Touch (*feel*) is attributable to Air.

107. So, we derive our five Sense Organs from the five Basic Elements of the Universe; and *my mind spins why most of the self-styled and so-called Gurus are exhorting us to get rid of this beautiful life after life, and telling us to curb our Sense Organs and shun all the bestowed divine pleasures of this beautiful existence, called LIFE.*

SERIES - 10

# Incarnations

108. An ordinary Human Being has more or less four Faculties *(kalas)*.

109. Those who are knowledgeable, intelligent, talented, and a visionary can be said to have eight Faculties; and are Greatmen (*Mahapurush*).

110. The moment, a human, a Man or Greatman, realises his/her Sacred-Self ie., attains *Bhagwatta,* he/she achieves *'Moksh'* and becomes *'Mukt'* ie., free from fear of death.

111. Those who realise their Sacred-Self, are then no ordinary and normal humans. They attain

divinity and virtually become one with the *Parmatma* ie., get connected to the conscious of the Universe.

112. The self-realised humans remain no ordinary man/woman; there is complete metamorphosis. Such people become magnetic. Miracles start happening in their day-to-day life. Even their inadvertent thoughts and wishes fructify effortlessly.

113. Lord Ram and Lord Krashn were very highly evolved humans who had realised their Sacred-Self in their life after life, and had thereby become one with the *Parmatma* for long.

114. Lord Ram had twelve Faculties and Lord Krashn had sixteen. To me, both appear to be one and the same. Anybody, who has more than eight Faculties, is deemed as an Incarnation of *Parmatma.* So far, Krashn has been the Highest Incarnation.

115. Lord Ram and Lord Krashn were real-time extraordinary personalities incarnate from epics.

116. The *maryadas* (demeanours & etiquettes) so meticulously observed and abided by Lord Ram were no mere empty preachings, but were rather a live demonstration of *dharm* in practice, without fear of any unpleasant consequences to the self.

117. Lord Ram had no malice against anybody; and kept the dignity and pleasure of all others above himself.

118. Lord Krashn too put the *dharm* (order) of the society above all other things; and that no costs were too high to save the society from *adharm* or re-establish *dharm* in the society, come what may.

119. The beauty of Lord Krashn was that He was not only very intelligent, calm and quiet; but would also always be very sweet and polite enough in all situations; and would quickly accept any eventuality without any bickering, and would forthwith move on to try and find out the way forward.

120. The Gita pre-existed Lord Krashn; and He had only reiterated it to Arjun in the exigency of the situation to wake him up from his

emotional upheaval and exhort him rise to the occasion for the protection/establishment of *dharm* (order) in the society.

121. No worthy and orderly society can exist without *dharm,* where, there is: Live and let others Live. Love and let others Love. Have Joy and let others rejoice too. Let Peace, Freedom, and Happiness be reasonably and equitably ensured for one and all.

122. Lord Ram and Lord Krashn are epitomes of humans' zenith. They are adorable, and worth emulations and worshipping; but, nonetheless, worship alone, per se, would not *ipso facto* do anything or take us anywhere. Were it so, there had not been need of such incarnations. And, Abhimanyu could not be killed the way it was done.

123. So, we have to correct ourselves, and start living a meaningful life; by adopting the demeanours and etiquettes of Lord Ram; and cultivating the static, calm, and peaceful mind with dynamic and restless attitudes, like Lord Krashn.

SERIES - 11

# The Worship

124. Some humans have been or are so good, extraordinary and outstanding by their thoughts, actions, demeanours, sacrifices, and styles of leading their lives that the common people on their own love and like them, and feel like worshipping them.

125. People consider such humans as their Ideals; and therefore start adoring, adopting and worshipping them.

126. An 'ideal' is a thing or state which is either very difficult or well-nigh impossible to achieve; it can be a person or situation.

127. Many a times, such humans are even idolised to immortalise them.

128. So far so good. It is trite to remember and pay rich tributes to such humans and keep them, their ideas and ideals, alive for emulation in future by generations to come.

129. There can be no issue or objections if such acts and occurrences partake the character of 'Worship'. Let their Pictures and Idols be placed in Temples and Memorials and worshipped; but, the mythical problem (illusion) arises when we start expecting miracles from the Name and/or Statue of such people, without any wish or even semblance to actually follow their demeanours and ideals.

SERIES - 12

# The Deities

130. I have said that the 'worship' to be meaningful should be the reverence of the reminiscences of the Great Men, so that we may try and emulate & imitate them in our life.

131. I have also said that there is nothing objectionable in even idolising the Great Men.

132. The 'Idols', when the parables of Myth and Miracle are attached to them, are called Deities.

133. Some Deities do in fact have miraculous powers, which leads to their deification.

134. The Deities get empowered by the visits and faith of their devotees by a metaphysical process, akin and analogous to *Reiki*.

135. Hence, more the visitors of a Deity, the more it is empowered; and older a Deity, the more powerful it is and its aura.

136. The power and aura of a Deity are not equally felt or experienced by all individuals. It depends on so many factors, such as, the purity of the persona; depth of devotion; the intensity of faith, &c. In *Ramayan*, Lord Ram could talk even to the herbs and shrubs about Sita's whereabouts.

137. A Deity can be anything and of any material. Eg., The Deities of Lord Krashn, Balram and Subhadra in the Jagannath Temple in Puri, are of wood.

138. The contemporary prominent deities of the day are: *Tirupati Balaji, Jagannath Temple* in Puri, *Vaishno Devi* Cave in Jammu, *Shirdi Sai Mandir*, &c.

139. I have had personal experience of acute elation and bliss, at-least at, and in the

whole premises of, *Jagannath Temple* in Puri. In *Garbhagriha* (sanctum sanctoram) my body-hair became erect and my eyes were wet by elation and bliss from the ether of the view and aura of Lord *Jagannath.* I have also got a wonderful experience at *Banke Bihari Temple* in Vrindavan. Once, when I had first time gone there with my children and we were rather stranded in the huge crowd inside the temple, a *Gosai* (Pandit ji) suddenly appeared before us, escorted us to the platform in the back portion and made us stand there right in front of *Bihari ji.* We comfortably watched *aarti,* he also brought *Maalas* and *Prasad* (bit of the *Bhog*) of *Bihari ji* for us from the front, and just disappeared.

SERIES - 13

# The Faith

140. The *'faith'* is anybody's confidence, or supposed dependence, of subsisting, achieving, or accomplishing something, owing to somebody, or due to doing or not doing something.

141. That somebody may be the so-called God, a goddess, a deity, a guru or even a man. Or can be something, like keeping fasts or performing some kind of rituals.

142. But: A 'faith' is a faith, is a pure faith.

143. A 'faith' is a belief, is a pure belief.

144. A 'faith' is a myth, is a pure myth.

145. Nonetheless, a 'faith' can be an essential requirement (even if not a need or necessity) and the biggest mythical support measure in humans' life; and has a great psychological potential of making them do wonderful things in life.

SERIES - 14

# The Bhakti (Devotion) and Prayer

146. I have, in essence, already said that a 'faith' is a complete myth and is nevertheless true and real, which also perforce applies to a 'prayer'; but there is something worse to prayer, because it involves begging. The Faith and the Prayer when put together can be called *"Bhakti."*

147. The faith and prayer are rather two sides of the same coin, with prayer on the tail side of it.

148. A faith is covert but when you let the cat out of the bag and express and assert your faith, it becomes overt, and called *'Prayer'*.

149. Ordinarily, the prayers are a sheer and colossal waste of time; and can at best be no more than the survival and effect of a ripple in the Atlantic of the Sky. However, the wish by 'Sacred-Self' or when made in a transcendental state during meditation, can shake the whole Universe for its fulfilling.

150. The prayer with heavy heart by a person in grief has no wings to fly and reach anywhere; and can at best be like the bursting bubbles in polluted waters.

151. *Bhakti* is a sign and symptom of Negativity in mind. More the Negativity, more is the Fear. More the Fear, more is the *Bhakti*. The cycle goes on, and its diameter and the frequency of its rotation increase to any extent with the growing Faith.

152. The *Parmatma* has made us out of Himself, after His own image and last imaginations, as His coequal, to love us and play with us, for His own entertainment.

153. So, He has divided Himself from Himself for Himself.

154. So, I am 'that' and my *Mann* is my sacred-self and real me and my stupendous body is His magnificent house for His comfortable stay and have liaison for enjoyment (*bhog*) of this beautiful wonderland and wondrous Universe.

155. We are completely free and independent and are governed unequivocally by the uniform Laws of Nature (*Vidhi ka Vidhaan*); and the Parmatma observes laissez-faire in this regard, blatantly and flagrantly.

156. So, when you, yourself, are that, where is the question of praying and go on *begging* from some unknown and imaginary figures and entities (the so-called Gods and Goddesses) in the Skies.

157. Nothing can cause more pain and pity to the *Parmatma* than seeing us so weak and begging all the time.

158. So, stop praying and begging forthwith. You are 'that'. Realise your true-self; and be a great doer. Always go on good-wishing and acting for others, the society and yourself as a good & great actor in the given situation and

occurring conditions, without any bickering or blaming anybody for such situation or circumstances .

159. A *'karmyogi'* is the one who doesn't wait for the fruits of his work to be happy, but enjoys his good work itself, similarly as a wicked person rather relishes planning and doing bad things to harm somebody.

160. But, we have to always necessarily observe and obey *Sanatan Dharm* (our Eternal Duty), come what may.

161. A hand which helps is holier than the lips that pray.

162. Please don't confuse Prayer with Worship. Former is Begging while latter is Thanking, whereas an *aarti* is a beautiful admixture of Prayer and Worship.

SERIES - 15

# The Death

163. We are 'that' and our mann is His reflection and a witness and evidence of His presence in us as our life.

164. We die when our physical body becomes incapable and incapacitated for inhabitation of 'that'; and our mann (ie. Atma) takes a flight out for a new abode for its boarding.

165. Our mann, on our death, carries with it all the knowledge and the memories of our lifetime, but not till its next birth.

166. The mann ie. our Atma can't get to its new abode until and unless it agrees and

passes through a tunnel of very sharp light (proverbial River of Fire) for its purification ie. for destruction of all memories and malice towards one and all. However, the intrinsic development (evolution) of our true-self remains intact.

167. But, some disgruntled souls dread the Tunnel of Light and refuse to enter it, despite counselling by the noble spirits on duty, including our ancestors *(Pitr);* or some may even dodge it.

168. Those who dread the Tunnel of Light and refuse to enter it are usually those who die suddenly or untimely in an accident and are, therefore, not able to realise and accept that they were dead. Such people may have to impudently roam in oblivion till the end of time, or till the time they somehow reconcile themselves and venture to pass through the Tunnel of Light.

169. This Tunnel of Light is in fact nothing but the Chamber of Supreme Consciousness (Parmatma), which is full of bliss and pleasure; but, it doesn't have the kind of real sensual pleasures, tangible comforts, and such actual

feelings of pain & pleasure or of emotions of love, &c as we the humans have and enjoy in this world.

170. Those, who manage to dodge the Tunnel of Light (albeit, exceptionally and foolishly, out of ignorance) may come back on Earth and take birth with memories of their previous birth, which may entail so many psychological disorders. The memories of previous birth would however fade with the passage of time.

(Today, I had decided to write, and had in fact actually started writing, on "Meditation"; but don't know how have I ended having written on "Death")

SERIES - 16

# The Meditation

171. I have stated in the beginning of this Series that initially there was nothing but Energy, which was conscious of being and monotony of feel of bliss and bliss alone.

172. We too are in fact nothing but the same consciousness.

173. So, we are 'that' *(Parmatma Himself)* but do also own this mortal, but magnificent, body, with amazing Sense Organs to enjoy and this wonderful world to tread about.

174. In fact, it is 'that' who created us by dividing Himself from Himself to play with, and enjoy Himself, in us.

175. But, in this celestial process, the happiness of the peace and unmatched pleasure of lasting 'bliss' are lost in oblivion.

176. The 'meditation' is the technique to reach to our pure consciousness (Sacred-Self), which is the nucleus of our *Mann*, and have rare and ecstatic experience of glimpses of our blissful Real-Self.

177. The meditation initially imparts us some mental ease, peace and/or general gut feeling of comfort and solace, as we get just the feel of presence of our divine-self in us.

178. Then we start getting momentary glimpses of our true-self, which exhilarate us, so that we intermittently crave for such excellent and exceptional experience again and again.

179. Then we one day have a real glimpse of our ethereal sacred-self, which makes us feel the never-before and unforgettable bliss.

180. Then we someday are able to identify ourselves with our divine-self, which makes us drown in bliss and bliss and bliss.

181. This is called "Self Realisation." But, if our divine-self *(Atma)* somehow connects with the supreme-self *(Parmatma)* and accidentally merges in it by failing to re-identify and recognise it, demerger is not possible, and such person will on Earth be declared as have died suddenly.

182. Then such person is *'that-as-a-whole' (Parmatma);* and can acquire any life-form, like incarnations do.

183. All of us are evolving, meditation or no meditation; and so is true for every life form.

184. Evolution means change. As a matter of fact, everything in this world is changing all the time. Change is the rule of nature. We are changing every moment.

185. Humans are the best creation on Earth, but they are the ones who are the least satisfied and most restive. That's the beauty. *That makes a man a 'man'.* The present day civilised and modern world owes its such attainments to the inquisitiveness and restlessness, and resultant requirements and necessities, of the mankind.

186. But don't ever think that all other life forms are only suffering. In fact, they are perfect in themselves and enjoying, and are fully satisfied too. Of course, their level of pleasure and suffering is far less than of humans.

187. Evolution takes place only during the life. Evolution in fact implies rise in one's level of consciousness.

188. The process of evolution consumes and requires energy which it imbibes from the ether of the Universe.

189. The meditation empowers and our every step towards self-realisation changes our mettle and makes us more and more susceptible to imbibing enormous energy from the Universe.

190. Thus, the meditation and the consequential self-realisation can do wonders in our life, but our 'freedom' remains intact; and we are still totally free to think and do whatever, good or bad, notwithstanding that we are a sacred-self.

191. More is the one pure and free from evil, more imminent the chance of his being sullied, similarly as the white and cleaner the clothes,

fairer is their inherent possibility of catching dirt.

192. I feel that the 'meditation' is not the same thing as *'yoga'*.

193. The *yoga* comprises physical, mental and spiritual practices, and projects 'self realisation' as very intricate and arduous *'saadhna'* (practice), which even an ardent seeker would feel very difficult, or rather well-nigh impossible, for him to adopt, practise and achieve.

194. The meditation, as I see it, is very very simple, the simplest thing to do; and it is in fact just a pursuit for disambiguation of our real- self.

195. All that an ardent seeker has to do is to move to a quiet corner of his or any house (I would not advise any open area wheresoever, even the hills or Himalayas. A 'cave' in the secluded hills can however be the best, which may nonetheless be not viable or practically possible) and aimlessly stay there effortlessly quiet in any posture which is most comfortable to him for doing or thinking anything, except sleeping. That's all.

196. Just do that, *Lo and behold,* you would automatically reach (attain *Bhagvatt*a), unknowingly and effortlessly. *More inadvertent, the quicker.*

197. So, the meditation leads to peace and yields empowerment, and the self-realisation is its fruition.

198. The meditation can be done in a lidded state, or even with open eyes, though I don't subscribe or recommend to the latter view as it appears to me very difficult, if not impossible.

199. I must caution, knowing and belief are not the same as experiencing a thing. Hence, the self-realisation is not a matter of knowledge or beliefs, but a reality, which has to be reached/ achieved and experienced, individually by meditation.

200. First, the meditation takes us to mere glimpses of our divine existence; then we have full glimpse of our true and sacred self; then if we are able to identify ourself with our real-self, we are self-realised and become free *(mukt)* from fear of death *(mukti).*

201. A *mukt* (liberated) person achieves *paramanand* (such persons are also called, *"paramhans"*, and realises his permanence and oneness with 'that', the divine.

202. But, rarely, someone accidentally drowns and merges with 'that', the divine, with his full wisdom and memory, and inadvertently attains divinity, which I deem a status, superior to even 'that', because of their subsisting worldly wisdom and experience.

203. Such persons, who attain 'divinity', die on earth, instantaneously, the moment they drown in 'that', but otherwise, they attain eternity and remain as celestial and ethereal entities, who can nonetheless acquire any live-form on Earth at will.

204. Such persons who attain divinity, when they come on Earth are called incarnation. An incarnation is impregnable and formidable. He cannot be defeated or destroyed by anybody, and not even by 'that' *(Parmatma)*. He can possibly be annihilated only and only by another incarnation, whereafter his edifice would vanish altogether and forever and lost into 'that'.

205. Some of the best paradigms of incarnations *(avtaars)* are Lord Ram, Lord Krashn, Lord Buddh, &c., whereas the worst instances are of *Dusht* Ravan, *Dusht* Kans, &c.

206. Some of the good paradigms of self- realised people are Vibhishan, Bhishm Pitamah, Vidur, *Gopi* Radha, *Sakhi* Draupadi, &c., whereas the Dhritrashtra, Shakuni, Gandhari and even Karn are bad instances of them.

SERIES - 17

# Draupadi, The Queen of Queens

207. I rever Draupadi above any woman character. I consider her the incarnation of the ultimate beauty and intellect, with an aura and eclat of fire.

208. Lord Krashn never remembered *Gopi* Radha, after seeing Draupadi whom He instantly accepted as His *Sakhi* (spiritual consort). His longing for her was unlimited, unmatched and unending.

209. I believe, the 'inpregnable' bond of Lord Krashn with *Pandavas,* was His *Sakhi* Draupadi.

210. I don't know if there is any temple of Draupadi, or of Lord Krashn with *Sakhi* Draupadi, anywhere in the World. Given a chance, I shall certainly do.

211. I shall elaborate upon my wondrous and inimitable heroine, *Sakhi* Draupadi, some other time.

212. But, by the way, contextually, I wish to speak out here on the issue as to who is responsible for the devastation of *Mahabharat*, Dhritrashtra, Duryodhan, Shakuni, Yudhishtar or even the sharp & saline Draupadi.

You may be aghast if I say, "None of them" but that's true.

The two persons who were squarely responsible for the catastrophe of *Mahabharat* were none else than Bhishm Pitamah and Karn the great. The beauty of the fallacy however is, both of them, fell foul of and literally stood with *'adharm'* under the illusion of their bounden duty. In fact, they knew not, knew not, and knew not.

213. Had they not stood on the side of Duryodhan; or had Bhishm freed himself from the ridiculous and egoistic shackles of oath of his bondage to the Crown, Duryodhan would never dare fight an adversary which had a mentor like Lord Krashn and a great archer like Arjun.

214. In the whole epoch, it is Draupadi, the most beautiful, sharp and attractive woman ever born, who made supreme sacrifice for the sake of elimination of wicked and eradication of evil from the society, knowing full well what was going to be the price, even as she could stop the fight.

215. Lord Krashn, on the insistence of Draupadi, had already apprised her about the outcome and horrendous consequences of the fight; and told her if she so wished, He could stop it from happening.

216. Lord Krashn had rather unexpectedly and unequivocally said to His beloved and kind hearted *Sakhi* Draupadi the bitter & ruthless truth that the whole *Kuru Vansh,* except her five husbands and five others, would vanish. Her own sons, father and brother would also die.

217. Naturally, the disgruntled Draupadi prayed to Lord Krashn to try and stop the fight. He agreed, but told her to take time and think, what would be the state of affairs of the commoners in a society where a powerful personality like her could be ill-treated, openly and so shabbily, and in front of the King and his courtiers like Bhishm, Vidur, and *Guru* Dron, with impunity.

218. But, see the unparalleled and divine greatness of *Maharani* Draupadi who, for the sake of protecting and establishing *'dharm'* (order) in the society, nonetheless made a very daring and extraordinary decision, over her own compelling reasons, insurmountable situation, self-interests, and suppressing her acute surging emotions of well-being, love and compassion for her father, brother, and even her own sons; and decided to let the fight take place. I don't think that there can be a higher paradigm of sacrifice.

219. There is a general and common belief that the seed of the genesis of *Mahabharat* lay in the so-well-known, unseemly comment of Draupadi, in jest, on Duryodhan, *"Andhe ka*

*Putra Andha"*, when he fell into a pond water, taking that to be a mere illusion.

220. Without disputing the veracity of the said clownish remark, attributed to Draupadi , I would say that it was not at least the whole truth, for the simple reason that the crooked and ingenious attempt to surreptitiously kill *Pandu-Putras* in *Lakshagrah* blaze happened when Draupadi was nowhere on the scene.

221. For a war, battle or a fight like this, there is never just one reason or factor; there is a multitude of factors, including the capacity and capability to fight, besides the attitudes.

222. Sometimes, a woman alone can factor in, as was the case of Queen Padmani and, to some extent, of Draupadi in *Mahabharat*.

223. But, we must remember that Draupadi stepped in only after *Warnavrat Lakshagrah* incident.

224. Devi Draupadi was born from the *Fire of Yagya* (Yagyaseni) and was extraordinarily beautiful with extraterrestrial glare, sharpness and intellect; and was easily a pride of herself and, of course, also of *Pandu-Putraas*.

225. The delightful *Devi* Draupadi, on the one hand fetched Lord Krashn closer to *Pandvaas* as, on the other, made Duryodhan an ardent envy of them. Karn was also quite upset and restless, and wanted to defeat Arjun at any cost, for no other reason, but just to break the 'pride' of Draupadi by proving his superiority over Arjun and his better eligibility and entitlement for her.

226. The said stupid jest of Draupadi *('Andhe ka Putra Andha')* would have definitely compounded the insult of Duryodhan and his clan in Yudhishtar's Court by their disarming at the instance of Draupadi, instead of punishing them with death, for pulling out their arms in his Court.

227. True that such arrogant and clownish remark of Draupadi, even if seen in isolation, could nevertheless drive a wedge between them at heart and a deep cavity of anguish in mind, which could cause some kinds of bitter skirmishes in future, but this was otherwise too flimsy to engage in a fight like *Mahabharat*.

228. Yes, of course, disarming in a public gathering, that too on a ceremonial occasion,

was too big an insult to be borne by any self-respecting individual, much less somebody of the stature of *Yuvraj* Duryodhan. Karn had in fact pleaded with Yudhishtar and preferred death to disarmament. He realised, such slur was worse than death.

229. With this standpoint, the people responsible the most, for the fight of *Mahabharat* were Draupadi, besides Shakuni and Dhritrashtra, who fanned the arrogance and ambition of Duryodhan over and above justice and the welfare of Hastinapur.

230. But, *notwithstanding the above germane factors, the Mahabharat, nonetheless, could never have taken place, without the constant encouragement and support of Karn for his own selfish reasons and inadvertent wrongful contrivance of Bhishm Pitamah.*

SERIES - 18

# The Miracles

231. This is a Scientific World. In other words, It's a causal world i.e., nothing happens in this world without a cause. There is also a cause for a cause of a cause &c.

232. When the cause of something or some event is unknown, unseen, unexpected or unexplained and shrouded in mystery, such wondrous thing or event is sometimes deemed as *'Miracle'*.

233. So, the assumed miracles are an illusion that has its seeds in mystery.

234. The mystery is something or some phenomenon that we do not know the name of or do not know anything about.

235. So, the miracles are nothing like that, but are some happenings which are unacceptable to us as ordinary or normal things or events due to our ignorance of, and about, their cause.

SERIES - 19

# The Nazar [The (Evil) Sight]

236. The so-called *'Nazar Lagna'* is not a pure myth. It is a stark reality; but is nevertheless a matter which is in the realms of metaphysics.

237. *'Nazar Lagna'* is a psychological attack on oneself by another person or other persons from his or their evil or dubious sights.

238. Our aura and thoughts, and so many other taints of our personality, are largely reflected through our eyes, besides so many individual body languages.

239. So, our eyes can talk more, and more intensely, than our tongue can ever do.

240. So, whenever two persons meet or see each other, there is bound to inevitably take place some kind of, intentional or unintentional, inadvertent and subtle give and take (exchange) through their eyes, which can more or less, profusely and enormously, affect the psyche of such persons, depending upon the quality and strength of their respective personas.

241. Such factors not only affect the persona and aura of interacting persons, but can even perceptibly change the climate, vibes, positivity, brightness and the fragrance in the vicinity of their presence by a ethereal process, which I shall like to call, "Human Magnetism".

242. I can vividly recall, I have experienced such ethereal flights at-least twice, once in the graceful presence of *Priya Darshani* Indira Gandhi in a marriage; and another at Dwarika in the company of *Prabhari* (The *Swami* who was incharge of the *'Muth'* in the absence of *His Divine Shankarachaya*). I also have similar experiences when in Muzaffarnagar on *Dushehra* Day, the Chariot of Lord Ram used to traditionally stop in front of our house, for a ceremonious recess with our family at our home.

243. The malady however is, that an Evil Eye affects the healthy, kind hearted, honest, pure and divine the most.

244. My sincere advice in this regard therefore is, carefully choose your friends, associates, and acquaintances; duration of meetings with them; and distance to be maintained from them in a meeting. This also perforce apply to the places you visit.

245. Similarly as the presence of some people moderates and optimises the vibes of a place and results in elation of the climate and atmosphere around them, the flip side is, vicious and vindictive people vitiate the happiness and serenity of the place wherever they step in.

246. These attributes of good and bad peoples are also inexplicably true for our belongings, especially our Car, Cattle, House, Shop, or any other property and premises.

247. Similarly as there is Evil Eye, there are Eyes that emit Blessings, Goodness, Love, Affection, and Bliss for one and all.

248. We must not visit dirty or viceful people or places, as also not closely involve with, or look deeply on, insane, lunatic, shabby, handicapped or unfortunate persons, and least the beggars, except helping them from a distance.

249. Such people and places would not only suck your *'shri'* (luck & positivity); but such people would, instead of wishing you goodness, also, more often than not, envy and curse you.

250. The *'nazar'* affects our psyche, as explained, which may then in turn reflect in us in so many psychological and/or psychosomatic bodily symptoms, such as heavy head, disorientation of mind, pale skin colour, general overall weakness, vertigo or tingling in the body.

251. It's a common knowledge, the *'zhada'* by burning dried Red Chillies, *Fitkiri* (Alum) or by Shoes &c, has inexplicably been found miraculously effective; I don't know how and why it works, may be it acts as an antidote, similarly as does the *'nazar'*.

SERIES - 20

# The Metaphysics

252. 'Metaphysics' is a very fine and subtle reality juxtaposed to Physics. It deals with things which are real but don't perceived.

253. In Ancient India, Metaphysics, the study of spirit and the ethereal energy, was quite advanced. But, today, in the modern world, it is a matter of *nescience.*

254. As a matter of fact, the *Nuclear Physics* is, strictly speaking, an offshoot of Metaphysics only.

255. Nuclear Physics deals with the Structure of an Atom, and it's fission or fusion, and the

immense energy that is thereby generated, can, besides the *Atom Bomb* and the *Hydrogen Bomb,* be also utilised for peaceful purposes through controlled nuclear reactions in *Nuclear Reactors*.

256. An 'atom' is the tiniest particle of an 'element', which comprises a Nucleus with so many Electrons rotating around the nucleus. The quality, properties and characteristics of an Element depend on the nature of the protons, which are found in the Nucleus.

257. Though an atom cannot independently exist or be seen by naked eye, it has all the properties and the characteristics of the concerned matter. There are 118 basic elements on Earth, such as Carbon, Iron, Gold, Hydrogen, Oxygen, etc; and everything in the world consists of them only.

258. Two or more atoms of an element, or of more than one elements, form a Molecule. Eg., one molecule of Oxygen ($O_2$) has two atoms of Oxygen (O); and two atoms of Hydrogen (H) with one atom of Oxygen (O), form one molecule of Water ($H_2O$).

259. A 'molecule' is the smallest particle of a substance which can exist independently, and has all the properties and characteristics of that substance. For example, each drop of water in a bucket, is the same as the whole water in it.

260. Now I come to the point. Everything in the Universe is interconnected; and everything in it affects everything else.

261. So much so, even our mere sight can affect Mountains or Oceans or, for that matter, any and every other thing, similarly as it does to other living being. There is a usual saying, "A sight can do break a stone." But, such changes are not visible because they take place at sub-molecular level and our eyes can't see inside the molecule as to what happened or is happening to it.

262. The changes which so take place are reflected by the changes in the behavioural patterns of electrons inside the atoms of the molecules, constituting the subject matter. The electrons may shrink and collect at places in their orbit, or start rotating fast or irregularly, or may even start colliding, resulting in self destruction.

263. But, at the same time, looking at it conversely, sightings by us of Wonderful Sky, Great Mountains, Infinite Oceans, Splendid Forests, Lakes like Mansarovar Lake and Pangong Lake, Rivers like *Ganga* and *Narmada,* and Exotic Animals and Flowers in the wild, even on Discovery or National Geographic TV channels, can do wonders to us and our attitudes in life. However, nothing on Earth can amuse a man and infuse a new life in him, more than sighting of a Beautiful Woman, and Love of a Woman of his choice, and vice-versa.

SERIES - 21

# Blessings and Good Wishes

264. So, the beautiful things in Nature and affable persons gratify and empower us without asking and even without any will or wish on their part, naturally.

265. We should therefore remain near them or go to them as often as possible.

266. Blessings and Good wishes are virtually the same.

267. Blessings and Good Wishes, when they naturally emanate from our Sacred-Self out of love, affection, regards or gratitude, the whole Universe is shaken and churns to fulfil our such wish.

268. The same is the position when a Curse naturally comes from someone's True-Self.

269. However, the intensity and effects of the same also depend on the eligibility (moral strength or vulnerability) of the blessed or cursed individuals.

270. Any Blessings, Good Wishes, or even a Curse have to naturally come, or be justifiably given, from the Core of the Heart to be effective and meaningful.

271. Any Blessings or Good Wishes, which are just a formality, or mere words, or are by a nonentity, or given to a undeserving person, are nothing more than a writing in sand on shorelines. Same is the position of a Curse, if it is sheer balderdash outburst.

272. So, most of the Greetings today are illusory and useless and are like strokes on water to try and create the maximum bubbles.

SERIES - 22

# Giving-Taking

273. We give things (besides Love, Affection, Respect, Regard & Help) to others out of Love, Affection, Respect & Regard or Compassion, let alone the selfish deference and considerations.

274. When we give something to somebody, have the feel of sweet pleasure (bliss) there and then; that's all about it. I don't see any reason why shouldn't one take pride in doing it.

275. But, if anybody expects something in return, in this world or beyond, nothing can be more ridiculous than that.

276. A charity is sans any sense of a feeling of giving, and is rather done to have eternal pleasure by feeling in us the happiness of the beneficiary.

277. In my view, there can't be any higher 'charity' than paying our taxes honestly and on time. Those who evade taxes are the biggest thieves, and culprits of the entire populace; and a slur on the nation.

278. Accepting something from somebody is a great art, and needs to be heeded. Most people accept a gift with pretended reluctance and with a sort of unnecessary Inferiority Complex, without any grace or applause, much less with thanks or gratitude, with which a gift ought to be accepted.

279. Some other people would even have the audacity to ridicule the gift before the guest in his face as to how useless it was for them, and so many other such things were already lying with them.

280. On the contrary, please imagine a situation and feel the pleasure of a guest when you open the gift in his presence and appreciate it;

or open the box of sweets brought by him in his presence, eat it, and say, "Oh my God, so tasty, really, thank you".

281. Similarly, when somebody comes to invite you for a wedding or any other function, if you open the Invitation Card immediately, appreciate it, and have a few pleasant words with the host.

282. Not caring of the guests, or not properly accepting their gifts, or not introducing them to the important people of the day, amount to undermining the guests, if not an insult to them.

283. Please remember, very big or very costly gift may also unduly embarrass the host.

SERIES - 23

# Balderdash of the Bogey of the Proponents of Peace, Contentment, Detachment and Inertia *(Mumukshutva)*

284. Peace is not the same thing as Pleasure. Restlessness is the sign of Life; whereas the Peace is a thing which is to happen only after death. So, let us not waste time and indulge in this mirage.

285. The *Parmatma* deliberately bestowed on humans all His faculties, save and except 'peace', and purposely made them very-very restive.

286. The 'man', where he is today, is only because of his inquisitiveness, dissatisfaction and resultant restlessness.

287. The contentment is not the same thing as fulfilment. Contentment would mean satisfaction with whatever we have ie., no further need or necessity ie., no more R & D or progress, since the Necessity is the Mother of all Inventions. People find ways to do what they have to or get what they need.

288. There can't be a worse nonsense than the peace theory of 'detachment'. Attachment to the self, and to our kith and kin and things, is but so natural that the very idea of not having attachment to them is *per se* pre-emptive and preposterous.

289. We get all motivation and impetus to do and achieve things in life from our attachment to the self and to our kith & kin only.

290. Our desired love for others; and duty & obligations to the Society and Nation, or even to the World at large, are altogether a different matter in this context.

291. Some people tell me, a person who achieves advanced stage of spirituality does not want anything or do anything ie., he becomes a *'mumukshu'*. I don't subscribe to

this nonsense vicious circle of idle-inertia at all. My experience is rather juxtaposed.

292. Self-discipline, sensibility and hyper sensitivity are however classic sign of higher consciousness, which if not recognised or cared, may rather unfortunately lead to insanity and idiocy.

293. I repeat, in a nutshell, the actual reality is:-

i) Struggle and Restlessness are 'Signs of Life';

ii) Satisfaction and so-called Contentment are virtual 'End of Life';

iii) Peace is 'Alien to Life';

iv) Rigidity is the 'Character of a Dead'; and

v) People become, *Saint, Sant, Sadhak, Sadhu, Yogi* or a *Muni* to either avoid the 'Rigours of Life' or to loot the Ignorant, Poor and Rich alike.

SERIES - 24

# Mahabharat and Gita : My Perspective

294. Lord Krashn was no doubt great and an ultimate incarnation. *Mahabharat* is however an interesting and remarkable story of Lord Krashn which in spite of his best efforts and intentions of establishing peace and *dharm* in the society met waterloo and ended in a fiasco. It is a saga of total failure of Lord Krashn and uncalled-for destruction and devastation, the worst and atrocious sufferers of which were blameless Gandhari and the decent Draupadi. The whole thing was a complete and evitable disaster.

295. The real culprit of *Mahabharat* was none else than unconscionable and reckless bettor Yudhishtra, who was let go scot free by Lord Krashn, with impunity; while Arjun was also all-through unnecessarily glorified. The heroine of *Mahabharat* was, of course, and no doubt, Draupadi.

296. *Gita* is in my opinion a discourse that virtually teaches us to stop living if we want to free ourselves from worldly sufferings. I don't understand what remains in life, if we detach ourselves from our love, emotions and all attachments.

297. Moreover, it's a book which is tedious to understand and impossible to practise. In *Mahabharat,* Lord Krashn himself recited *Gita* to Arjun; but Arjun repeatedly doubted and refused to accept its discourse, till end and until Krashn made him believe by overawing him by his mythical *Virat Swarup*.

298. I certainly understand that in the exigency of the occurring circumstances and the situation, though the nervousness of Arjun was natural, yet laughable, and his demeanour was absolutely preposterous, which necessitated

his brain-wash to save him and his clan from disgrace at any and all costs, since *'upyash'* (disgrace) is worse than death.

SERIES - 25

# Karmayogi (Workaholics)

299. One thing that everybody must try and learn from Lord Krashn is that we should fail not in doing what is our *'dharm'* (duty) to do in the given situation, irrespective of the damage or sacrifice it may involve; and we must do away from the stubborn and stupid *dharm* of Bhishm or of Yudhishtar.

300. Both, Bhishm and Yudhishtar, adopted a myopic approach and took the *'dharm'* as fixed and defined canons, dehors the time, situation and circumstances, and ended in doing so many *'adharm'*.

301. If anybody asks me to name only one person who were responsible for *Mahabharat*, I would straightway name Yudhishtar, without any hesitation, besides Bhishm and Karn; and Shakuni and Draupadi, the least.

302. So, the point is, don't ever shackle yourself in any myths and prejudices, contrary to your conscience and innate sense of justice in a given situation.

303. The weak and wonky people would hardly do anything or take any responsibility on them of even themselves, what to talk about of others; and shall rather deem their preposterous and ceaseless worship, deep and hallucinating *bhakti,* and endless prayers (as beggars) as enough 'debt' on the so-called God for multiplied redemption in future in their this life, and beyond, knowing not that they were only boring, annoying and antagonising the *Parmatma,* by wasting their precious time and stupendous faculties bestowed on them by Him for the pleasure of Himself in us as we.

304. The assumptive or hallucinating mythic faith and beliefs of such people are naturally bound to be broken, sooner or later, resulting in their temporary disgust and distrust in 'God' but they would soon reconcile that there must have been some defect or deficiencies in their worship of the 'God', and would restart, instead of rather realising their own folly in not doing the needful.

305. Anybody who indulges or engages himself in an occupation or a calling of his liking and interest, enjoys his pursuit and such engagement. His work will be his entertainment and he would hardly be ever tired of his work. Hence such persons would be bound to succeed and excel in the area and fields of their respective interest. Such people naturally and *ipso facto* become a *"Karmyogi"* and can also be appropriately described as 'workaholics'.

306. So, you can succeed and excel, more often than not, only in the areas and fields of your interest and liking. Hence, wherever or whatsoever you are, and if you find your area or field of operation is not of your taste,

you should, as far as possible, immediately switchover to the venture of your interest.

307. Thus, a *Karmyogi* does not focus or wait for the outcome of his work and efforts for his happiness, but remains happy throughout while doing and enjoying his work itself, without so often drifting his attention or diverting his energy more to ponder about the results. Naturally, such people would on their success and accomplishment be not merely happy but their joy be rather compounded beyond imagination.

308. So, let us be a *Karmyogi;* We should not waste our time and energy in balderdash pursuits, like worship, *bhakti* & prayer, but consider work as worship and service to the society as our redemption (offering) to *Parmatma* for His having created us.

309. As of now, even the *Parmatma* is flabbergasted by the superlative excellence and wonderful achievements of the mankind. The *Parmatma* has the knowledge of the world only as much as we do.

SERIES - 26

# Sukh-Dukh (Pleasure & Pain)

310. There is intrinsically nothing like Pain or Pleasure. They are relative terms and mean differently to each person depending on individual's fact-situation and circumstances.

Eg.- A person who doesn't have a four-wheeler, gets an Alto Car, he would become very happy and the pleasure of him and his family would not know any limits; whereas, a person who is driving a Mercedes Car, has to somehow sell his Mercedes and instead buy a Honda City, he and his family would be very unhappy or rather sink in depression.

311. The Pleasure & Pain have to co-exist like day & night and light & darkness. The Concept of

Pleasure owes its occurrence to Pain. Pleasure & Pain are two sides of the same coin, namely, our *Mann* (Mind).

312. The 'mind' doesn't exist in *presenti*. It is always in the past or in future and never in *presentia*. It always goes on roaming in the past and simultaneously goes on weaving a network for future; and the present is constantly and instantly converting into the past.

313. I have already said, *Parmatma* has made us very capable and independent, and wanted us to be very restive and enterprising, so as to be self-sufficient and able to live and enjoy life like a 'king'.

314. So forget about controlling your mind or having peace ever till death.

315. But, you have a better and an excellent alternative to Peace ie. start living and enjoying life in *presenti,* so that your present entertainment becomes your *presentia* which, in turn, instantly goes to your mind as your past and generates happiness, and the cycle goes on.

316. Conversely, diseased and depressed Mind commences a vicious cycle of Pain and Sufferings.

317. So, please try and be always positive, happy and cheerful as far as sensibly possible in a given situation; and also try to shorten and minimise the period and impact of sorrow and sadness, because that won't take you anywhere or serve any purpose except to devastate you, may be completely.

318. Which is why :

   (i) Misfortunes never come alone;

   (ii) Our worst fears come alive; and

   (iii) We are advised on the death of a kith or kin, not to ever prolong the period of mourning, but to rather shorten it and save a festival or any other auspicious occasion from falling within the duration of mourning.

319. But all said and done, Pain and Pleasure would come and go, you wish them or not, similarly as bad times do come, even when nobody desires them.

320. But, nevertheless, one thing is entirely in your hands (read, control). You can shorten the period and impact of your sorrow & suffering to a minuscule by ignoring them and still continuing and enjoying life as usual; or you can elongate and prolong your sorrow & suffering endlessly, or even unto the end of your life, if you think and involve in them endlessly, or sink yourself in grief, forgetting, you are "that" who created you for His own pleasure and play, in you and as you, and nothing else.

321. The *Parmatma* has created us, by separating Himself from Himself to love and play Himself with Himself by being Himself in us, who is reflected in us as our '*Mann*'.

322. The purpose of life is nothing but only to live and enjoying. But, there could ever be no Pleasure without Pain, as already explained, *supra*.

SERIES - 27

# Brahmcharya (Celibacy)

323. In common parlance, *'Brahmcharya'* is abstinence from "sex"; and appears to be a very simple and routine kind of a thing.

324. But, if we go deeper, it is a very subtle and difficult proposition; and is much more than what meets the eye.

325. The sex has infinite craze and energy. The *brahmcharya* is the art and exercise to divert this energy to any other pursuit by abstinence from sex.

326. But, mere keeping away from sex or sexual affair would do or achieve nothing, and

would rather boomerang, unless and until such person is able to be sex-neutral from within and immune to all external sexual stimuli and erotica, which, in my view, is next to impossible in the modern world.

327. The conservation of sexual energy by celibacy in fact occurs because of absence of the sexual stimuli and thereby stopping of the actuation of formation of sex hormones and other ancillary and auxiliary things and materials.

328. The energy so conserved and saved can then perhaps be utilised elsewhere in the system of our body for any other desired purposes.

329. But, otherwise, in my view, the *brahmcharya* is an absurd and unnatural idea that militates against the Laws of Nature; and is an antithesis to the inherent principle of progression and progeny.

330. Sex is the seed of 'Live Kingdom', be it *botanical* or *animate kingdom;* and is the perceptible feel of the tantalizing and unbeatable, ultimate sensation that permeates the whole world.

331. The whole world is so sexy and sex oriented that, for once, it appears to have been created by *Parmatma* for sex and sex only.

332. The sex is too strong an urge to kill or control, because it is divine and a direct attribute of the *Parmatma,* which is loved and liked by Him. An 'abstinentee' may ostensibly appear to be very graceful, but he may in fact be a hidden sex-maniac, you know not.

333. I would therefore always advise not to ever try *brahmcharya,* but to rather constantly go on releasing all such pent-up energy in order to maintain and have a balanced and healthy *psyche,* free from vices.

SERIES - 28

# Love and Sex

334. Love is a phenomenon, while Sex is an essential and deliberate act of routine nature; but both have a huge and pronounced *pineal* impact on our body and mind, and psyche. The whole animate world revolves around sex, and 'mating' is a recipe to have and enjoy its unique divine pleasure.

335. The sex is a basic instinct and is the seed/ recipe for progression and progeny of all species in the world, plants and animals alike.

336. The fools deem this boon of boons as sin of sins, and have virtually made it a taboo. So much so, even husband-wife, sometimes,

more or less, suffer with some kind of a guilt in their intercourse.

337. My body is for me for my enjoyment through the amazing equipments and senses provided to me by my body, called Sense Organs.

338. Our five important sense organs are : Eyes for Sight, which is an attribute of Fire; Ears for Sound, which is assumed to be an attribute of Sky; Nose for Smell, which is an attribute of Earth; Tongue for Taste, which is an attribute of Water; and Skin for Touch, which is an attribute of Air.

339. The most interesting and exhilarating thing is, all these five Sense Organs are also, simultaneously, more or less, our Sex Organs, with folds of our skin, wherever epidermis ends and meets internal membrane, the most.

340. Ideally, there should be an absolute and complete freedom of "mutual" love & sex; and any restriction or embargo on 'mutual love & sex' is wholly unnatural, unrealistic, total nonsense, blatant cruelty, and a sin of the first order.

341. But, nevertheless, the craze and lust for sex is inevitably so intense and irrepressible, it has to be essentially contained forcibly by law, besides the stringent social and religious sanctions and other written or unwritten taboos, in order to set-up a coercive system in the society against having forcible sex, and also to rein-back mighty, high-born, or higher-up from indulging into *'vyabhichaar'* (promiscuity and infidelity).

342. It is a stark reality, this is a *'mathuni shristi'* (sexy world). In other words, nothing live would survive long, be it vegetation or animals, including humans, without sex.

343. Sex is not only indispensable, but is also the most beautiful and attractive *'sha'* (thing) in this world, which invariably attracts our attention. That is why, it is generally there, this way or that way, in every 'advertisement', though may be wholly irrelevant, much less required.

344. Without sex, there wouldn't be any fructification in Vegetative-Kingdom and neither any offspring in Animal-Kingdom;

and the whole live-world would soon meet its waterloo and be extinct forever.

345. So, the importance and omnipresence of sex in this world and to us cannot be overemphasised.

346. Humans are capable of enjoying the sex of lowest level or of highest order; or both and in between.

347. The primitive sex is had by animals lower than mammals; while the mammals, other than humans, have sex of the lowest level only or so; but the potential of *humankind* to enjoy the sex knows no limits.

348. The women inherently have far more sex than men and their potential to enjoy sex is also accordingly. Let there be no misconception in men on this score.

349. Most men sleep with woman all the time just to satisfy their biological lust and lust only, without any element of love or emotion. This kind of physical sex is of the lowest level and is in fact of the kind of animals.

350. The humans are characterised by their understanding, love, and emotions, and sans them, they are no better than animals.

351. Love means natural attraction, emotional understanding and bonding, which results in friendship or a relationship. Be it with a man or woman.

352. Once such friendship between a man and a woman takes a romantic turn, it becomes magnetic and magnificent *(Ishk)*. Nothing more beautiful can happen in anyone's life, if such romantic attraction for each-other is genuine and equally from both sides.

353. The moment such attraction pulls each other towards each other and becomes their passion to be near each other, they wouldn't know when their love became erotic, demanding them to physically come closest to each other, as if they wanted to amalgamate into each other.

(There is a story that once Lord Krashn amalgamated with Radha, and became *Radha Roop: Radhavallabh* Temple, Vrindavan, near *Banke-Behari* Temple).

354. The emotional and passionate sex (intercourse & coitus) of this kind can't be mere lust, and is certainly holistic and of highest order.

355. Such intercourse is divine and identifies & introduces the true & sacred-self of each other, to each other.

356. So, if the sex originates from love, it is very beautiful and divine; but when it arises from mere lust, it is terrestrial and of animal kind.

357. The sex, in spite of being essential and inevitable, is nonetheless also an evil because it has the potential of devastating the graceful fabric of a civilised and decent society, if left unrestricted, and not suitably controlled and regulated.

358. But, it is for sure, if the sex is in any way drastically suppressed, it is bound to boomerang in so many ways, bodily & mentally, and by way of compulsive promiscuity & infidelity, like fornication and adultery.

359. Marriage is one most secured, satisfactory & decent solution, which also instantly solves all other consequential and related issues.

360. Poligamy and Polyandry can also help control promiscuity and infidelity among oversexed people in the society.

361. But, what about those, men or women, who are single for whatever reason? What is the solution of their sexual deprivation; and other sexually obsessed sex maniacs?

SERIES - 29

# Prostitution

362. Prostitution, commonly known in India as *'Vaishyavritti '* is a notorious profession, yet it's the oldest profession of the world.

363. It is on the face of it, or rather ostensibly, very bad, unholy, unhealthy and even nauseating.

364. So, many of us would feel crestfallen, if I describe prostitution as a noble profession of sorts and compound it by saying, a prostitute deserves reverence in an elite society; as also do deserve the sweepers.

365. In India, the prostitution, as a profession, is virtually prohibited by law; and it is also a taboo for a long time now, not because of its futility or undesirability but out of sheer hypocrisy and empty idealism at the national level.

366. I must clarify here, prostitution is banned in India only as a profession. One-on-one transaction between two adults, without involvement of a third person in the transaction, is no offence under the law, unless it amounts to 'adultery' in a given case. For example, in Haryana, any couple who may not be husband-wife, can freely stay in any govt. public resort or accommodation, without hassles of any kind.

367. Shorn of all other things & details, the net visible effect of closure of sex markets and of ban on prostitution is that this menace has spread, albeit camouflaged and unidentifiably, in the midst of the whole society, and is mostly running as call-girl rackets or in hidden whore houses. They have the audacity of even advertising in the national dailies under various modes and ways.

368. The other natural, but very bad and highly deplorable, repercussion of ban on prostitution is abundant increase in the cases of adultery, infidelity, fornication and of even incest and rape.

369. So, I earnestly feel, the existence of sex-markets and prostitution is necessary and inevitable, simply as we can't do away with drains; and if we try and do that, dirty water would pull back into our houses and pollute our homes.

370. Hence, we cannot do away with the indispensable dirty drains, but nevertheless we can sanitise them, keep them clean and maintain them free from stink and any kinds of infections or we can even cover them. The same is perforce *(mutatis mutandis)* applies to prostitution.

371. In other words, the prostitution must be recognised as an honourable profession, should be totally an optional enterprise, regulated by licence and its terms & conditions, such as the locations, frequent medical checks and standards of general and personal hygiene, etc, etc. I believe, there is no dearth of excellent

paradigms in this regard from all over the globe.

372. But, please make no mistake, I am not even for a moment suggesting, much less recommending, the trafficking in women (or man). If anybody is found indulging in the trade of 'trafficking in women' or forcing or inducing a woman into the profession of prostitution, he or she should be dealt with an iron hand and sentenced with most stringent & exemplary punishment.

373. As on today, the age-old profession of prostitution appears to have met its waterloo in India, when it has in fact only ceased to be a profession, but has otherwise clandestinely spread all over.

374. Now, the handicaps are officially called 'differently abled'. Similarly, the prostitutes can be known as 'city women'.

375. I deem the prostitution a novel & noble profession, because she gives her whole (surrender her mind & body) to cater the requirement of her client and satiate his eternal and natural sexual urge, which is a

unique service that no other professional on Earth does or can. It's a noble job, because it not only keeps her clients in good stead, but also, in turn, possibly save the society from many social sexual evils and vices.

376. Please pardon me, if you don't agree. You have full right to differ or severely criticise me, and present a 'critique' on what I have said hereinbefore.

SERIES - 30

# The Mujra

377. The word *"mujra"* is one of the most miserably misunderstood word; and is very unfortunately wrongly associated with prostitution.

378. Prostitution is for those who feel deprivation or remain insatiate from sex; while the *mujra* is for the elite who are so satiated with sex that they are fed up with such entertainment.

379. The *mujra* was at its best in the Court of Royals by their courtesans for their, and their courtiers' recreation and redemption from boredom.

380. Besides the art of singing and dancing of these pretty & curvy women, their courtesy and courteous demeanour used to be *par excellent*. So much so that the elites would send their children to them to learn manners and etiquette.

381. A *mujra* in fact epitomized performance of decent acting & dance with soothing & lyrical singing on classical music by these beautiful, erotic and curvy women, which would often take the audience-viewers into a new world of spiritual romance at ethereal heights.

382. In *mujra,* some people could even experience the excellent & extraordinary eternal bliss of their true and sacred-self.

383. I got insight to write like this about *'mujra'* from an interview of an old *'tawaif'* of a *'kotha'* in Lucknow on Door Darshan long time back, who not only told so many things about the reality of *'mujra'* which were already obliterated by the dust of oblivion a little too soon, but also recited a spiritual *'nazm'* and explained it.

384. In this context, you may, inter alia, refer to the *nazms* of the famous Hindi Films, *"Pakeezah"* and *"Umrao Jaan"*.

385. The *'mujra'* had subsequently trickle down to lower and lower standards among masses; and alas, it were now virtually extinct.

386. Now the *'mujra'* stands replaced by cheap Cabarets, and 'Item Songs' in Cinemas and TV.

SERIES - 31

# Hindu Marriage and the Riddle of its Customs and Traditions

387. A Hindu Marriage is a sacrament (religious ceremony), unlike a *Nikah* (Muslim Marriage) which is more of a contract in nature.

388. The Hindu Marriage *Sanskar* (process/ procedure), till 1955, before the codification of the customary Hindu Law of Marriage by the *Hindu Marriage Act 1955,* at the instance of Prime Minister Pt. Jawahar Lal Nehru, much to the chagrin of President Dr. Rajendra Prasad, was very intricate and intriguing.

389. Before this Act, the Hindu Marriages used to be very often disputed on the ground that it

was not properly solemnised, which at times created unseemly hassles.

390. Now, under the Act, (i) A Hindu Marriage may be done as per the customary rites & ceremonies of either party; and (ii) If such rites and ceremonies include *"Saptapadi"* (ie. taking seven steps by both of them jointly before sacred fire), the marriage becomes complete and binding with the seventh step.

391. Now, under the Act, in order to facilitate the proof of marriage, the Registration of Marriage is also provided for.

392. The marriages among Sikhs are performed under *The Anand Marriage Act 1909.*

393. The inter-cast marriages are not permitted among Hindus, even under the 1955 Act.

394. However, the inter-caste marriage of an Arya Samajist Hindu is valid under *The Arya Marriage Validation Act 1937,* even if done before this Act.

395. Moreover, The Hindu Marriage Act 1955, shall nevertheless apply to such Arya Samajists as well.

396. An inter-caste marriage can also be done in Court (Court Marriage) under *The Special Marriage Act 1954*; but then in that case, Hindu Laws shall cease to apply to them, forthwith.

397. Hindu Law is a *personal law* ie. it is not *Lex Loci*. It means, it travels with us wherever we go, irrespective of our migration from place to place.

398. It's not that the *Muslim Personal Law* doesn't have any good features. It has so many good concepts, such as *Mehr* (Dower Debt), *'Muta' marriage, Iddat,* etc.

399. The 'marriage' is an excellent internationally recognised instrument and device that has beautifully institutionalised the sex, to bonk and play it cool, besides the bonhomie of a home, as we all know.

400. Our forefathers were prudent and right in the matter of marriage of their children. 13-14 to 15-16, or even less, was the usual age of marriage of boys; and 12-13 to 14-15, or even less, used to be the normal age for marriage of girls. Thus, *they were least deprived or bereft of sex and sexual pleasures, right from the age of puberty,*

*leaving little avenues to them for self-abuse, which tremendously helped in their holistic growth.*

401. The common refrain for late marriages is the career. Let them be "first settled in life".

402. The people don't understand the significance of sex and its exhilarating effects on our mind & body. They lapse such natural pleasures of life for better material comforts in latter part of life which, in my view, is a soul-destroying perspective of leading life. They know not, the sex is the elixir and spice of life.

403. As of now, the minimum prescribed age for marriage of girls and boys is 21, which should ideally be the maximum age for marriage, after their attaining the age of majority at 18.

404. Before I solve the riddles of the customs and traditions of a Hindu Marriage, I wish to strike a note of appreciation about some of the rituals in Hindu Marriages.

405. i) *"Ring Ceremony"* provides the bride and bridegroom an opportunity to touch and have a feel of each-other, possibility with an

eye-to-eye contact as well; and the mutual exchange of rings is virtually parting with mementos.

ii) *"Haldi Ceremony"* serves a dual purpose: One, checking of the bodies of the bride and bridegroom by the *'Naayan'* (wife of family hair-dresser) and *'Naayee'* (family hair-dresser) from each-other's side; and two, removal of contagious infections and prevent their mutations in each-other's families.

iii) *"Ghurchari"* (Horse-ride with a band or drumbeat) in the streets of the city, is a loud announcement that so & so is getting married, should anybody has objection.

iv) *"Varmala"* appears to be yet another opportunity to the bride to verify and in case of doubt, not to go ahead.

v) *"Pheray"* is an interesting ceremony of registering of solemn commitments by the bride and the bridegroom to each-other, before the sacred fire and in presence of audiences (witnesses) of either side. And,

vi) The play of *"Kangana"* which is conducted between the Bride and the Bridegroom, first at bride's place and then also in bridegroom's, plays an important role in establishing an early rapport between them, besides the entertainment of all those who are present on the occasion.

406. In ancient times, the marriages might mostly used to take place either by 'abduction' or by forcible obtention or by winning in a battle and donation of daughter or sister to winner by the defeated, along with so many other valuable things, in order to have some kind of a permanent relationship with the mighty winner.

407. The Customs & Traditions that the Hindus religiously and dogmatically obey and perform, to the best of their ability and capacity, are virtually of the kind, which clearly match to a marriage of a daughter or sister by a defeated father or brother.

408. I really wonder or am rather inconceivably and irreconcilably surprised, how and when we the Hindus voluntarily and proudly adopted the Customs & Traditions of marriages that they

were once obliged to perform in the marriage of their daughter or sister as a defeated party; and my such dilemma is further compounded and confounded, how come and why the Hindus even now take pride and religiously follow those obsolete and obtrusive customs & traditions.

409. Be that as it may, but that's why, and how it comes, that the one who gives his daughter or sister in marriage nevertheless bows down to the bridegroom's side.

410. But the Question is why do so even now? Who is bigger and higher, donor or a taker? If the answer is obviously, "donor", then why do we, nonetheless, still have honour and take pride in bending before the in-laws of our daughter or sister.

(I had very clearly mentioned in the 'Matrimonial' of my daughter, "we believe in equality of relations").

411. This (The obsolete 'sensible' legacy, which is now redundant and a total nonsense, and is alive today as absolutely preposterous customs & traditions) also explains why

the Bridegroom still carries a sword and his friends and relatives walk alongside with weapons during the *'Ghurchari'* and *'Baraat'* processions.

412. This is why the mother and sisters on *Ghurchari* pray for the win & welfare of the bridegroom and he necessarily visits a temple before proceeding further to 'win' the bride.

413. The Sisters-and-Daughters' Husbands *(Damaads)* are requested to walk in front of the marriage procession with the bridegroom to show their solidarity with us, because they are more powerful than us since they had already once defeated us earlier; and for this, they are also honourably treated and handsomely rewarded throughout the marriage, till the bride is brought home.

414. The *Baraat* didn't straightway enter the city of the bride for fear of being surrounded and beaten. It used to stay in Jungles on outskirts of the city *(Junglevaasa)*, and only the *Naayee* and *Brahmin* would go into the city to inform the bride-side about the arrival of *Baraat,* and report back about the conducive situation.

415. The *"Junglevasa"*, has become *'Janvaasa'* over a period of time, but its tenets remain the same.

416. The *Baraat* would venture into the city for marriage only after the *'Nyotany'*, an important ceremony, in which all those members of the community, who matter, come to welcome and honourably invite the *Baraat* to the venue of marriage.

417. This also explains why the Bridegroom rides a horse or a chariot in the *Baraat* and carries a sword, and his friends and relatives too keep their weapons with them; and, being winners, they proceed to the venue of marriage with great gaiety and jubilation and even with obtrusive pomp & show, besides some vulgar brag & boasts.

418. The height of nonsense and preposterous conduct now-a-days is, and how come, that the *Baraat* in the high-end marriages would reach the venue of the marriage or the bride's place, escorted by a posse of hired men, attired as Mughal Soldiers and weaponry, and march in with an equally inappropriate and obnoxious song, exuberating Mohammedan Ethos.

The irony is this that with this, the bride's side sits on cloud nine and the parents, relatives and friends proudly present the bride, surrounded in a semicircle with bridesmaids, before the *Baraat,* for further matrimonial ceremonies.

419. Such re-enactment of the ancient kind of a Mughal marriage, doesn't exhibit even a semblance of an arranged or a love marriage, or of even a voluntary marriage to the winner by the defeated; but it rather deplorably canvasses a paradigm of a heinous and forcible marriage by a mighty Muslim with a hapless daughter or sister of a helpless Hindu.

420. I am surprisingly surprised that such stupid and obsolete, yet so strong and nostalgic, are our classic and archaic customs & traditions of Hindu Marriages that they are still obeyed, to the extent possible, in their minutest details. Eg.- When the bridegroom appears for '*Dwarpooja* Ceremony' at the bride's place for his welcome and '*Jaimala*', the maids of the bride's family refuge to desist and welcome him, and retort with choicest teasers (called "*seetnays*") in a jest to avenge the defeat and denigration of their master.

421. The *kalgi* (brooch) of the *pagdi* (headdress) of the bridegroom is retained by the bride-side as a memento and proof of relationship with the bridegroom-side.

422. The *Baraat* is treated well and with full honours throughout their stay during marriage, till the *Baraat* with bride's *Doli* (Palanquin) is safely escorted till the border of the city, and bid apologetic adieu.

423. So, please wake up and be restive and pensive.

SERIES - 32

# Astrology, Palmistry and the Like, We Believe in or Believe not

424. Science means study of, and acquiring knowledge of, cause-and-effect relationships.

425. Hence, another feature and characteristic of science would *ipso-facto* be its capacity and potential to make predictions.

426. There can be *'abstract science'* ie., pure science, which is based on theories and theorems.

427. There can be *'applied science'* such as discovery of a pointy nail on the principle of difference between "force" and "pressure".

428. Then, there are *'empirical science'*, such as "astrology" and "palmistry", which are straightway based on direct and concrete experience on ground.

429. And lastly, there are *'social science'* or pseudoscience, such as Sociology and Political Science, where the predictions are no sure shot, but are in the realms of mere tendencies.

430. *So, the Astrology and Palmistry are worthy of being called "empirical science".*

431. Let me explain it very simply. If 'A' with planets XYZ positioned in his horoscope @ JKLM died in a particular manner, place and time; and the same thing similarly happens with 'B' and 'C' too, then in that case, it can reasonably and logically be predicted to happen with 'D' as well in an identical planetary placement in 'D's horoscope. The same logic would also *mutasis mutandis* apply to Palmistry.

SERIES - 33

# Physics

432. The 'physics', unlike as the name suggests, is the study of energy; and is more a matter of Science than Nescience.

433. All matter is in fact energy only. In other words, there is nothing but energy.

434. The whole existence is a dance and interplay of energies and their synergies with the chemistry of the Universe.

435. There are four basic energies, namely, Heat, Light. Sound, and Mechanical ie., the physical force.

436. The other two energies are Magnetic and Electricity or Electronic energy.

437. Atomic energy is merely an offshoot of Heat; Solar energy is an offshoot of Light; and Hydal Power Generation essentially uses the force of velocity of flowing water; and so does a Wind Mill that of the air.

438. The most striking and stupendous thing about the "energy" is that one kind of energy can be converted into another kind of energy; and given the quality, efficacy and viability of the technology and the equipment, the input and output are commensurate.

439. Thus, the 'Sun' plays a pivotal role in running the cycle of life on Earth through the process of the agency of the plants called photosynthesis.

440. This apart, how all or any energy can be converted and utilised as Heat, Light, or Mechanical Force etc is a matter of study of Physics.

SERIES - 34

# Yantra, Tantra, Mantra

441. *'Yantra'*. The *yantra* here does not mean an instrument or equipment, but very typical structures/drawings/images made on a piece of paper, metal or of glass.

442. Hence, a *yantra* is a visual device, and depends on 'light' to be effective.

443. The charismatic image of a *yantra* reaches our brain through the optic nerves in our eyes.

444. This is how a *yantra* can obtain desired results for or to a person.

445. So, in a lighter vein, I can say, beware of the eyes of the other persons, especially of women, and particularly of beautiful women, lest you should contract the ailment of *"Ishq"*, which is not only highly contagious, but is also untreatable.

446. Comedy apart, *yantra* can be used by experts and individuals alike to obtain various kinds of results and benefits for themselves or others.

447. The most well-known and popular *yantra* is *'Laxmi-Yantra'*.

448. The *yantra* is more effective when coupled with *mantra* or *tantra* or even with both of them.

449. *'Tantra'*. The *tantra* relates to *"tan"* ie., our body, especially our whole nervous system; and depends on 'heat' to be effectively used.

450. *Tantra* uses various gestures and postures of the body ie., as in yoga. It is very effective when done in sharp sun or in front of intense fire.

451. Sex and sexual postures before the burning fire at night are very effectively used in *tantra.* Sometimes, it takes the full night; or night after night.

452. The same effect is sometimes obtained or increased tremendously by slapping hard the cheeks or/and buttocks of the woman/ women (who are used as tools) by palm or a cane.

453. Thus, our extremely heated and excited nervous system becomes very sensitive & susceptible and quickly picks up our desire or objective from our brain (read mind) and cosmically fulfills it very fast.

454. Early or untimely orgasm in either or both individuals of the couple may waste the whole exercise and frustrate the enterprise.

455. This kind of endeavours can at times take the couple to extreme orgasm, and may even kill the couple or any one of them.

456. This is a very vast and intricate subject, which is understood and dealt with differently by different people.

457. The tantra is more effective when coupled with *mantra* or *yantra* or even with both of them.

458. *'Mantra'*. The *mantra* relates to *"mann"* ie., our mind, as contra-distinguished from the term brain, which is of course the hardware of the intangible and unseeable, omnipotent mind.

459. *Mantra* works through 'sound'. I think, it would work harder, if simultaneously recited together by more & more number of people. Louder the better.

However, I feel, using loudspeakers will not be advisable; and should best be avoided as far as practically possible, in order to rid distortion of voice, and the bad or adverse effects that may therefore follow.

460. A *mantra* is a very subtle set or combination of words in any language in a poetic tone and manner.

461. A *mantra* is best written and composed in *Sanskrit,* because of its most scientific grammatical characteristics.

462. I have already said, *mantra* relates to *mann.* I have also already said elsewhere, *mann* is me; and that the God ie, *Parmatma,* is in me as myself.

463. So, the *mantras* can do wonders to us.

464. Hence, the *mantras* can also provide wonderful therapy to mental ailments.

465. A very astonishing thing is, our mind can fetch anything, yes, anything and everything, to us, without any act or action by us, merely by wishing, but it must not be a wish of a 'beggar', yet may be, an inadvertent wish of a *"faquir"*.

466. Please excuse me for my uncharitable remark here. Today's man is far worse than a Street-beggar, praying (read, begging) all the time, need or no need, day and night, 365 days a year.

467. I have already explained elsewhere in great details, the God created us to enjoy and play with us as His coequal, and He really drowns in sorrow and actually weeps to find that He

had, by and large, rather created an army of beggars among us.

The *mantra* is more effective when coupled with *tantra* or *yantra* or even with both of them.

468. Thus, *'Yantra' 'Tantra'* and *'Mantra'* together as in case of *yagye,* or jointly and severally, provide unique scientific tools to achieve magical powers and do things magically to ourselves or to others.

469. Such magical powers can be acquired for good (+) purposes or with bad (-) objectives.

470. The good magical powers result in bliss and grace; while bad ones give rise to evil and a devil.

Such bliss or grace is always used by Great-men as their blessings for the welfare of others and the society at large (It can be termed as *"white magic"*).

471. These powers, good or bad, are liberally known as *'tantric powers'* and those who practise such powers are called *"tantriks"*.

472. Even the white magic is at times misused for self-gain or personal gratification in terms of money or otherwise, including womanising, which leads to gradual evaporation of such powers and ultimately ephemeral effacement of them. Not only this, such tantriks may have also to suffer many other undefined evil consequences.

473. The negative (-) *tantric powers,* which are acquired with bad objectives, are used to captivate the evil forces, and use them for destructive purposes such as harming or killing some identified individuals (It is generally known as *"black magic"*).

474. Such (*tantric*) magical practices, be them white magic or notorious black magic, are a criminal offence in India.

475. I earnestly feel that this aspect of reality of *'Tantra'* should be revisited and scientifically researched at the government level. Even the rustic *tantriks* can be invited and hired for this purpose.

476. Please permit me to conjecture, Lord Shiva is the ultimate master of *"tantra"*; Hanuman ji

too is a great master of *"tantra"*; and *Shirdi Sai Baba,* among so many others, was also no less a white magician.

SERIES - 35

# Ram, Hanuman and Hanuman Chalisa

477. *'Ram'*: Here, in these lines, I don't intend to speak about Lord Ram, nor do I have capacity to do that.

478. However, serendipitily, I do have some insight about the word *"Ram"*, without even going into the etymology of it.

479. The word *'Ram'* is greatest and encompasses anything & everything in it, and the beauty is, it contains even "nothingness" in it.

480. The word *"Ram"* comprises two letters *'Ra'* and *'Ma'*. When we pronounce, *"Ra"* our whole mouth opens to the maximum; while, when

we pronounce, *"Ma"* our mouth is totally shut in nothingness, our lips are so tightly closed that even the air can't pass through.

481. When anyone pronounces the letter *"Ra"*, he/she is immediately connected to the whole Universe and can imbibe the energy of the whole universe, much less this mundane World alone.

482. With the inevitable follow-up pronouncement of *"Ma"*, afer *"Ra"*, the energy so imbibed, gets locked in us, with all its characteristics, holy or silly.

483. The quantity and quality of the imbibed energy of the universe would however depend on so many factors:

   1) The person himself and the purity and capacity of the person;

   2) The place and serenity of the place; and

   3) The day and time of the day.

484. However, nonetheless, I do not at all recommend *'jap'* of this word *'Ram'* (Cf. Lord *Ram*).

485. The word *'Ram'* should always be pronounced comfortably and completely;

1) Silence, vacuum in mind, and closed eyes, is in my view the best state;

2) The best time in routine life is the time immediately after we rise in morning; and any time of the day in good mood whenever we can 'inadvertently or leisurely do it;

3) The best places under the sky are any serene places: roof-tops, gardens, river banks, seashores, forests or hills.

486. Pronouncement of this word, two-to- there times at a time, is enough. It can be done silently or aloud, singly or collectively in a synchronised group.

487. Of late, I have thought and decided to also comment briefly on the *'jap'* of *Shri Ram Naam.*

488. Shri Ram Chandra, son of King Dashrath, was the incarnation of *"Ram"* ie., the whole-thing (universe) invested in Him.

489. Shri *Ram* looked simple and sober, yet very charismatic and magnificent.

(Shri Ram was in fact omniscient and omnipotent, which powers, He never depicted, unlike Shri Krashn)

490. But, one thing I must immediately highlight here. Contrary to common belief, Shri Ram was very strict and unforgiving. He would never forgive anyone for his follies. Forget it not.

491. Each of us have a little bit of *ram-tatva* in us. To put it more simply, it is so, similarly as a drop of water of a ocean has the same properties & characteristics as that of the entire ocean.

492. So, believe me, there is literally nothing which anyone of us can't do which Shri Ram could do (read, 'did') in His illustrious and inimitable life.

493. While a chant of the word *"Ra-am"*, immediately connects us to 'Ram', the whole, while chanting *ram-ram-ram-ram* &c appears to me to be ludicrous. The same is the position of going on writing ram-ram-ram all the time, note-book after note-book.

494. Thus, the purpose of worshiping *Shri Ram* is, and must be, to remember and to remind to ourselves the illustrious & magnificent life of Shri Ram, so that we may imbibe and inculcate His ideas, ideals, greatness and deeds in ourselves, without unnecessarily and superstitiously mesmerising ourselves with expected miracles.

495. That is how, it is good to utter or remember the name Shri Ram, to keep a *Ramayan* at home and read it daily or so often, to go to the temple of Shri Ram everyday or so often, or holding *'Ram-Lilas'* as frequently as possible.

496. Hanuman ji, who is supposed to be incarnation of Lord Shiva, was a born *'tantrik'* and had enormous strength and astonishing magical prowess.

497. Hanuman ji was not taken by Shri Ram with him, when He departed from this world; and he was left behind here to help the weak and hapless.

498. So, Hanuman ji likes, loves, and profusely blesses all those who help & serve the poor, weak and the hapless. I don't want to comment

here on healthy & wealthy *'yachaks'* (beggars).

499. The *"Hanuman Chalisa"* is rather a poetic story of Hanuman ji, depicting and demonstrating that nothing is impossible in this world and anything can be achieved and accomplished by faith and efforts. In other words, "where there is a will, there is a way".

500. So, it is rightly advised to the people in trouble to read the *'Hanuman Chalisa'* again & again, umpteen number of times, so that they are able to catch and imbibe the unfailing moral of it.

501. But, alas, most of us deem this great piece of poetry as a magical tool to please, or rather oblige, Hanuman ji, and ridiculously expect their problem after problem get solved as if it was a "magic wand" of Hanuman ji.

SERIES - 36

# Worship and Prayer

502. 'Worship' is totally distinct and different, to all intents and purposes, from praying.

503. Worship is an expression of gratitude to *Parmatma* and an exercise for graceful self-empowerment; while praying is simply "begging" to achieve or get things effortlessly.

504. Worship includes both, *'Yoga'* and *'Tantra'*.

505. *Yoga* is an internal practice of uniting with the whole *(cf. physical yoga exercises)* and includes "meditation", which is in turn the best and highest form of *yoga*.

506. *Tantra* is an external exercise and comprises use of techniques to control and manage the interplay of various energies within and outside us.

507. *Yagyas,* worship of 'Statues' and 'Images', *Aartis* etc are all examples of practices of *Tantra.* An *'aarti'* is, however, a poetic expression of a beautiful admixture of worship and prayer.

508. I have already said, the worship leads to the purification and empowering of our "self", with the result that 'miracles' start happening in our life; and all that, big or small, we wish or need for ourselves or for others is attracted to us and starts flowing to us automatically.

509. Now, the question is what a 'prayer' fetches to you: do I need to tell you, what you give to a beggar (as alms), compared to your loved-ones. Same is the situation here.

510. CAUTION ABOUT WORSHIP:

1) Worship is a very important and serious business. Do or not, no problem.

2) Worship normally involves *"tantra"*.

3) Please don't ever take *'tantra'* lightly or practise it casually. It can do unthinkable & incalculable damage to your health, wealth and welfare.

4) Go to a temple, fresh and well dressed only; and stay & relax there as long as you can afford.

5) Always take to a temple your choicest and distributable sweets and/or fruits only as a *'prasad'*, if any, and do distribute most of it there itself.

6) Try and participate in *"aarti"* whenever possible.

7) Never indulge in any *pooja* (worship) without being attentive.

8) Using any *'mantra'*, especially the *Gayatri Mantra*, as a Call-Bell; or playing it casually, while attending to other daily chores, or without being attentive to it, or while driving, or continuously; and the like, is not good or may be disastrous to your health and well-being.

9) We must not evoke or invoke the divine energy unnecessarily without being

receptive. It is akin to inviting a guest, with nobody to welcome him.

•——•⁘•——•

SERIES - 37

# Wish

511. A "wish" simplicitor is only a desire; and a mere wish is certainly, not a prayer, and neither the worship.

512. A solemn wish, which is neither a prayer nor the worship, works at a different level, has the capacity to move mountains; and has the potential to compel the universe to yield anything & everything.

513. So, keep wishing for yourselves and others genuinely and generously.

514. Any ill-wills would however always boomerang and recoil on ourselves.

515. This phenomenal world of today, is the net outcome of our solemn wishes and goodwills, and followup actions and activities.

SERIES - 38

# The Ghost

516. There can be a great deal of debate whether a 'Ghost' *(Bhoot-Pret)*, a Spirit, or a Soul (ie. the *Atma*) are one and the same thing or are different concepts. In my view, they are synonymous, but are used differently in different situations.

517. I have already stated elsewhere that real me is reflected in me as my mind. It is this real me in myself which survives after my clinical death.

518. Thus, after an individual's death, his mind nonetheless survives, as sullied or tainted (good or bad) as it may be...

519. If anybody's mind on death is as pure and untainted as it originally was, his spirit joins, there and then, with the whole ie., the Universal Consciousness (which, in my view, can be called, "*godhood*") and thereafter, such people take birth at will, and as 'incarnations' only.

520. Those individuals, who are in their life-time able to realise their true-self, do not on their death face any difficulty in their way to reincarnation, because they rush to the Celestial Tunnel of Fire to Eternal Life fearlessly and unhesitatingly, or rather hilariously, and get appropriately reincarnated, almost immediately.

521. Those individuals, who don't ever even try to know their Sacred-Self, much less realising it even a little, dread towards going to the Tunnel of Sacred Fire, and only on being persuaded by the appointed self-realised souls reach there in due course according to the weight of their respective sins.

522. However, those who never accept that they were dead and fail to be persuaded to march towards the Tunnel of Fire, join the clan of

similar people, called *Bhoot-Yoni* or *Pret-Yoni* (World of Dead), and lead a life of starvation till eternity, until they are liberated by their pious descendants by their good deeds.

523. Once someone passes through the Tunnel of Fire, his entire memory is destroyed, except his spiritual evolution (ie., the Evolution of his Soul), with the result that such individual becomes entitled to rebirth, on his turn and as per his entitlement.

524. If somebody is able to reach to the other end of the Tunnel of Fire and even join the Queue of Rebirth, without entering into it, such person shall take birth with memory of his previous birth, which would however fade with the passage of time.

525. The Ghosts have their own abode in a different world where they live an entirely different kind of life, which is akin to our life in our dreams.

526. In fact, the Ghosts, in the beginning, experience acute starvation, which passes out with the fading of their memories of this world.

527. I tried hard to peep into the queer world of spirits to know more about them, but nothing could come out from their cool world, except noisy silence, for want of any mutual communicating tools. I shall definitely share my knowledge about it, if and when I succeed in my venture in this regard.

528. But, there are still some individuals who are not able to even join the clan of spirits and remain aloof, in a group or all alone, either due to their strong attachment to something or someone or being held captives by some *witchcrafts practitioners.* It is these people who are in common parlance called *"bhoots"*.

529. The places where the presence of *bhoots* is experienced, are identified as 'haunted'.

530. A spirit vibrates at a very high frequency and thereby rarity the air around, making it cool enough to be felt by us. Thus, the presence of a spirit can be noticed by cooling and some mild to wild commotion in a limited area.

531. A spirit can be good or bad. Accordingly, good spirits can be used by a witchcrafts practitioner for good purposes; and bad ones

are used to practise 'Black Magic' for wicked and unholy objectives.

532. Stray spirits can however be troublesome and difficult to handle. They can't move far and wide on their own. They have to ride somebody (normally, man or a woman) to move around. Such affected person would feel very tired but could do strange things.

533. When a person dies, his or her spirit remains near his or her body and his or her belongings for quite some time; and may even freakily sometimes ride a beautiful woman or an handsome man, as the case may be, while his or her body is on way to cremation/burial ground.

534. I have reason to believe that a genuine witchcraft practitioner can treat such beleaguered persons.

535. I believe that the plight of a departed soul is over, once it reaches to the 'Celestial Tunnel of Fire to Eternal Life' or even to the 'Abode of Spirits'. But, the stray souls need to be helped out.

SERIES - 39

# The (Indian) Wife

536. The wife has no parallel and there can't be a 'home', much less an ideal home, without wife. She is a marvellous and maverick ergonomic personality.

537. A wife is all-in-one for her husband when it comes to caring. She plays the role of a constant companion of all seasons, as a friend, mother, nurse, homemaker, or even of a prostitute (frank, active, erotic and artistic) while it comes to sex.

538. The motivation and the stamina for such unique care and efforts come from the love and regards she has for, and from, her husband,

without which all the care she does would be mere duty being done out of compulsion only. The same would *mutasis mutandis* apply to the husband as well.

539. So, the wives should always be treated with love and respect; and the home and the house should always be deemed to belong to her, and she should never, in any circumstances, even for a moment, be made to feel that she had no right in them.

540. If there is no love and affection between husband and wife, the problems are inevitably bound to crop up between them. So, whenever any one spouse or both of them realise this, they should simultaneously assume that their matrimony has irretrievably broken and should immediately take steps for a decent and dignified separation.

541. When you look from outside, a home is a house. Otherwise, it is an enjoyable and happy place, where you can live, laugh and grow; where you are loved, respected and cared for; where you feel comfortable and have intimate relationship with some personal space; where you experience the healing component,

physically as well as psychologically, that it belongs to you (cf. the accommodations of which you are not owner); and above all, where the family members, especially the husband-wife, happily submit to each-other in deference to each other.

SERIES - 40

# Epilogue and Epiphany

542. In this concluding chapter of my Series, I propose to highlight and enliven some salient postulates of the series.

543. What is all about ?

There is nothing except "energy" which is conscious and has the sense of its existence.

544. All 'matter' is nothing but energy; and therefore even the dead matters have some consciousness and react to external stimuli, but their reactions/responses can't be perceived by naked eyes, because they take place at a sub-molecular level.

545. All happenings are nothing, but an interplay and dance of various energies from the realm of oblivion.

546. Who am I ?

I am nothing but consciousness.

547. Besides this mortal tangible body, my "real- self" is my consciousness of me. Real me is myself and is reflected in me as my mind, which is what would survive my death.

548. Things simply happen, you would never know why. No amount of logic or reasonings can explain them. So don't blame yourself or anybody else for them; or ever waste time in trying to know, and continue with your acting. It is like as in the 'Game of Playing Cards', a player can't know with any amount of effort why has he got any particular cards in a 'deal'; but playing those cards is wholly in his own hands. We have to simply accept happenings and situations as they occur, and try to always act sensibly. That's all.

549. The "life" is to live. There is no other purpose of "life" except to 'live'. So, don't waste your life anymore, live & let live fully. We don't know, if we were already in 'heaven' and were nonsensically wasting our life on this beautiful planet, to rid it, for eternal bliss elsewhere.

550. I don't think that the eternal bliss can in any way match the variety of our pleasures and happiness on this beautiful planet. I believe, the *Parmatma* has created us to break His own monotony of so-called eternal bliss and enjoy the life of love and play in us, as us, and with us.

551. As already stated and explained, God has separated Himself from Himself to love Himself. *That's the oneness of all of us !*

*I would wish you all to live a 'mast' life on this beautiful planet with optimum indulgence of all of your five senses.*

*The meaning of life is*
*to find your gift.*
*The Purpose of life is*
*to give it away.*

*- William Shakespeare*

# NOTES

# NOTES

*ज़िंदगी में **ज़िंदगी** ढूँढना ही ज़िंदगी है...*

***Life is to find LIFE in life...***